BUILDING LEADERSHIP

CAPACITY FOR

SCHOOL IMPROVEMENT

BUILDING LEADERSHIP

CAPACITY FOR

SCHOOL IMPROVEMENT

ALMA HARRIS AND LINDA LAMBERT

Open University Press
Maidenhead · Philadelphia

Open University Press
McGraw-Hill Education
McGraw-Hill House
Shoppenhangers Road
Maidenhead
Berkshire
England
SL6 2QL

email: enquiries@openup.co.uk
world wide web: www.openup.co.uk

and

325 Chestnut Street
Philadelphia, PA 19106, USA

First published 2003

A catalogue record of this book is available from the British Library

ISBN 0 335 21178 X (pb)

Library of Congress Cataloging-in-Publication Data
Harris, Alma, 1958–
Building leadership capacity for school improvement / Alma Harris and Linda Lambert.
p. cm.
Includes bibliographical references and index.
ISBN 0–335–21178–X (pbk.)
1. School improvement programs – England. 2. Educational leadership – England. I.
Lambert, Linda, 1939– II. Title.

LB2822.84.G7 H35 2003
371.2'00941–dc21

2002042580

Typeset by RefineCatch Limited, Bungay, Suffolk
Printed in Great Britain by Bell & Bain Ltd., Glasgow

CONTENTS

CONTENTS

CONTRIBUTORS' NOTES

Alma Harris is Professor of School Leadership and Director of the Leadership, Policy and Improvement Unit at the Institute of Education, University of Warwick. She has published extensively on the theme of leadership and school improvement and her latest books include: Harris *et al.* (2003) *Effective Leadership for School Improvement*, Routledge/Falmer; Harris (2002a) *School Improvement: What's in it for Schools*? Routledge/Falmer; Harris (2002b) *Leading the Improving Department*, David Fulton Press. Her most recent research work has focused on effective leadership in schools facing challenging circumstances and the relationship between teacher leadership and school improvement. She is currently working with the DfES, National College for School Leadership, General Teaching Council and NUT in a research and development capacity.

Linda Lambert is a Professor Emeritus and the founding Director of the Educational Leadership Center. She has been a teacher, leader, principal, district and county professional development director, coordinator of a Principals' Center and Leadership Academy, and designer of four major restructuring programmes. From 1989 to 1993 she worked in Egypt to set up a National Curriculum Center, and in Thailand and Mexico in leadership development. She is the author of several books including: *Developing Sustainable Leadership Capacity in Schools and District*, *Leadership Capacity for Lasting School Improvement*, *Building Leadership Capacity in Schools*, *The Constructivist Leader* and *Who Will Save Our Schools: Teachers as Constructivist Leaders*.

FOREWORD

BUILDING LEADERSHIP CAPACITY – SIMPLE, COMPLEX, PARADOXICAL, NECESSARY

[A] distributed perspective focuses on how leadership practice is distributed among positional and informal leaders as well as their followers. Understanding how school leaders work together, as well as separately, to execute leadership functions and tasks is an important aspect of the social distribution of leadership practice. [Such a] distributed view of leadership incorporates the activities of multiple individuals in a school who work at mobilising and guiding school staff in the instructional change process.

Rather than seeing leadership practice as solely a function of an individual's ability, skill, charisma and cognition, we argue that it is best understood as practice distributed over leaders, followers and their situation.

(Spillane *et al.* 2001)

Introduction

This is a difficult foreword for me to write. I will explain!

A few years ago I encountered an article by Linda Lambert setting out some of the key principles from her book *Building Leadership Capacity in Schools* (1998). It spoke powerfully, and so I used it with groups of students on the Masters programmes on which I was, at that time, tutoring at the University of Cambridge. It resonated for them, too. Here was a view of leadership that accorded with the aspirations of those school leaders, who were seeking to learn together about leadership and school development. It was a view that combined morally purposeful intentions with enquiry processes, learning models and a belief in the capability of all to contribute to leadership. But it was a view, too, that worked against the grain of the prevailing views and the myths of modern headship – we were, after all, at that point wedded to the idea of the hero head or 'super head' as the solution to underachieving schools.

It is always difficult to know how far one's ideas and practice is influenced by a book such as this, or how far it is the case that it fits with one's values and with the stage that one's own thinking has reached. Probably it is a little of both. Certainly, the most potent educational texts that I have read have made an impact more than just intellectually. The best educational theory moves us emotionally and practically as well as educating the mind. They are dynamic in the sense of changing practice.

Linda Lambert's book, when I acquired it, did just that. It was also one of the first publications that we acquired at the National College for School Leadership when the group that I was then leading was formed in November 2000. The first research programmes that we undertook, significantly, were focused upon capacity building (Hadfield 2002), distributed leadership and new models of leadership learning (www.ncsl.org.uk). The first 'context research' that we commissioned was a study of successful leadership in challenging contexts, and one of the key findings was as follows:

> Effective leaders in Schools Facing Challenging Circumstances (SFCC) are able to combine a moral purpose with a willingness to be collaborative and to promote collaboration amongst colleagues, both through teamwork and by extending the boundaries of participation in leadership and decision-making.
>
> (Harris 2002)

To return to the opening statement, it is hard to write this foreword for two reasons:

The first is a straightforward and very human one, and it is envy that Alma Harris had the vision to collaborate with Linda Lambert to produce a version of her book customized for the UK. I wish that I had had that idea, albeit that it would not have been accomplished so well! Perhaps that is the highest praise. If you have not encountered this text before, read it – all of it. It has powerful implications for our schools.

This is a wise book, an informed book and one that speaks authentically to school leaders. It is written by academics, but two academics who are also genuinely practitioners. Both the ideas and the ways in which they are expressed have a resonance and an accessibility that tell us this book was written not to aggrandize the writers, but to speak to the readers. The case studies of practice are a further illustration of a desire for closeness to the realities of our schools and classrooms.

This is an important book. Read it.

The second reason is that I have lived with the ideas and examples in the original publication for a few years now, and some of them are also part of my own thinking – or perhaps they always were. So, it is hard to disentangle the derivative from the original in what I will go on to write – which may, of course, be the ultimate homage!

In seeking to write this foreword I want, certainly, to pay respect to the quality of this outstanding book, but also I want to problematize it – to reflect upon how beguilingly simple and idealistically alluring the notion of distributed leadership is, but how inordinately complicated the implications are for implementation. It is hard to change accepted practices and norms within our schools. What a profound leadership challenge it is to take us there. To be fair, Alma Harris and Linda Lambert address this, too. In exploring both the complexities and the opportunities that redesigning schools as 'organisms' rather than 'organizations' can bring, the implication is that it is not easy – but the scenarios and case studies presented are, understandably, optimistic.

However, the current model for the school system in this country is not marked out by characteristics of learning, innovation, enquiry and knowledge creation. The talk has been more of structures, job descriptions, targets and performance management. It will involve new ways of thinking about how schools function and not always within a climate that is conducive. Professional learning communities are distributed leadership communities. They are also trust-based and socially cohesive communities. When community, cooperation and collaborative learning are the prevailing metaphors driving our schools, rather than hierarchy, competition and accountability, then it will follow that issues of voice, participation, ownership and active democracy will be the precursors of new leadership patterns, and this is a hard road to travel. It is one that journeys against the grain.

In the remainder of this foreword, then, I will attempt to pay homage to the ideas presented in Alma Harris and Linda Lambert's book by embracing them, exploring some of their themes and by reflecting on the complexities and paradoxes of living out some of those themes in the real world context of schools!

The paradoxes of implementation

While there is an expansive literature about *what* school structures, programmes, roles and processes are necessary for . . . change, we know less about *how* these changes are undertaken or enacted by school leaders.

(Spillane *et al.* 2001)

It goes without saying that if we want things to change then they cannot remain as they are. So, we will not achieve models of wider distribution for leadership without a redesign of the concept of school as organization. The paradox here, though, is that we are also unlikely to achieve this necessary redesign of schools without distributed leadership as the engine and capacity for change. This conundrum is very similar to the more widely understood 'structure–culture paradox'. Can we achieve change in culture without changes in the structure of schools? Will we be able to implement effective new structures without prior change to the culture?

There is a second paradox. Recently, a colleague and I were asked to identify some schools visited during our travels that we would recommend as locations for the study of distributed leadership. When we analysed the schools that we had put forward, what we discovered was that each of them, in different ways, was led by a visionary, charismatic, deeply committed and unusually idealistic headteacher. The paradox: it appears that the strength of will, vision and values-base required to transform schools as they are currently organized into contexts in which leadership is truly distributed requires strong headteacher leadership.

There are other issues, too, as confounding as these paradoxes, and they relate to:

- the way in which leadership is allocated or bestowed;
- the direction in which leadership travels;
- the language that we use to describe it;
- the metaphors, conceptual frames and mental constructs that inform our understandings of what leadership looks like and how it is lived out – constructs held by both leaders and followers.

Most complex of all, perhaps, to address are the belief systems that tacitly influence our actions. (Believing that everyone can contribute to leadership is as profound a mind shift as believing that all children can be intelligent and successful learners.) Those beliefs alone can change schools.

Beliefs that inform our thinking about distributed leadership

In developing a distributed perspective on leadership, we moved beyond acknowledging leadership practice as an organizational property in order to investigate how leadership might be conceptualized as a distributed practice *stretched over* the social and situational contexts of the school.

(Spillane *et al.* 2001)

As Alma Harris and Linda Lambert have persuasively argued, distributed or dispersed leadership is central to capacity creation – they have conclusively established that. However, I have also suggested that this distributed leadership cannot happen if schools stay as they are. This section explores quite how profound this might need to be in practice and its implications for change in schools.

Despite more than two decades of writing about organizational learning (for example, Argyris 1976; Senge 1990, Louis and Kruse 1995) we are still in a position of needing to develop understandings about what leadership really involves when it is distributed, how schools might function and act differently and what operational images of distributed leadership in action might look like (Spillane *et al.* 2001).

There are some basic questions we need to ask in order to clarify thinking and to offer a basis for debate. Some of the key questions would seem to be the following, and, having set them down, I will go on to discuss each of them in turn:

- What do we mean by *leadership* when we are talking about distributed manifestations?
- What are the organizational implications?
- How might distributed leadership operate in practice?

- What is the role of the designated 'leader' – the headteacher – in distributed contexts?

What do we mean by distributed leadership?

Leading is an enacted activity. It is a doing word. It exists only through its manifestations. It is profoundly inter-personal (can you lead without others?) and exists via direct impact upon or exchange with others, or through their perceptions and interpretations of leadership actions. When we talk with teachers about their headteachers, for example, they describe what he or she does, how he or she relates with them or others. They are as preoccupied with what leaders do as with the rhetoric of what they say. They want to see the talk walked!

Leadership is more complex than leading. It is as much akin to potential energy as it is to kinetic. Leadership is about the latent as well as the currently lived and enacted expressions of leading. As metaphor, it has much in common with the notion of intellectual capital – the poten-tially banked and available capacity to be drawn, and the interest that can be added! As such it potentially exists very widely within an organization – an argument power-fully made in this book.

Leadership, as we have come to understand it, does not exist in a literal sense. It is an enacted variable, dependent upon interactions between leader, 'follower' and context. If it did exist, as a trait characteristic, independent of fol-lowership and context, then effective leaders could be assumed to be equally successful whatever the situation. The history of football management in this country tells us that this is not the case! If, then, leadership does not reside in one person and is not independent of context, what is it?

Looked at from this perspective, leadership can be seen to be located in the potential available to be released within an organization. In essence, it is the intellectual capital of the organization residing (sometimes dormant or unexpressed) within its members. The role of the 'leader' in this scenario is to harness, focus, liberate, empower and align that leadership towards common purposes and, by so doing, to grow, to release and to focus its capacity.

The logic of this argument takes us to another problem posed earlier. If leadership is a shared function, and if it only expresses itself with and through others, how is it denoted? Who 'allocates' it? How is it 'distributed'? Intriguingly, when analysed in this light, growth metaphors become important – and the organizational implications are profound, because, first, its increase in capacity terms cannot be about key, hierarchically highly placed leaders getting better – it is not about training the few. It is about creating the spaces, the contexts and the opportunities for expansion, enhancement and growth among all. In fact, as will be discussed later, the old management structures are a deterrent, a debilitating frame.

Second – and this is a crucially important concept – it cannot be either imposed or assumed. Leadership has to be bestowed, denoted wilfully by those who are to be led. We accept leadership. We *allow* ourselves to be led, just as we allow ourselves to be coached. It is a reciprocal and dynamic relationship.

As such, and third, it cannot be delegated either. One of the myths of distributed leadership is that it equates with delegation. It does not. Delegation is a manifestation of power relationships. Expansion of leadership is about *empowerment* – opportunity, space, support, capacity and growth. Jobs and tasks are 'delegated' (passed down a managerial structure) but leadership is invitational.

As so far described, distributed leadership capacity can be seen as being an amorphous concept. Its purposefulness (and its accountabilities) comes from tightness around values (shared beliefs), moral purpose (the urgency to act and to achieve together for higher order purposes), shared professional capital (the combined and shared and expanding knowledge-base) and the social capital (relationships and trust). As Sergiovanni writes (2001), schools need to be culturally tight and managerially loose. Teachers and other school workers respond much more to their values and beliefs, to how they are socialized and the norms of their work group than they do to managerial controls.

So, *values* make leadership tight. There are, though, other key concepts to the distributed capacity dimension of leadership. One is the idea of *synergy* (discussed in Chapter 1), allowing fluidity and flexibility between people – variable leadership patterns and flexible teams. Another is *directional alignment*, moving this distributed function towards common aspirations and goals. Yet another is *linguistic alignment* – utilizing new organizational metaphors and appropriate language (elsewhere, I have described distributed leadership, for example, as being 'the space between the pebbles in the jar'). A final one – central to the capacity definition used in this book – is *sustainability*.

One last concept is *wilful professional emancipation*. Such distributed leadership patterns not only liberate leadership, they are emancipatory for the person in the professional. Those who work in schools give of who they are as well as what they do. The release and expression of potential through leadership creates the context for personal as well as professional realization. Leading the growth of leadership capacity is thus an intensely human and social process – deeply emotionally and spiritually intelligent. Tending to leadership capacity is a caring and authentic business.

What are the organizational implications?

Leadership is multi-directional. It can function down an organization, can grow up an organization or can operate across an organization. While this concept is both basic and obvious, our current organizational and managerial norms only readily facilitate top down leader behaviours. Problems occur in both vertical and horizontal directions of travel.

Paradoxically, the most complex and difficult form of leadership for dispersed and capacity building models is that which operates down through management systems, because it then becomes entwined with power relationships and role responsibilities. It is not that leadership and power are incompatible, but, having noted earlier that leadership has to be bestowed, power (or authority) does not necessarily facilitate this – the right to lead has to be earned, granted by the followers. So, as leadership cannot be imposed, the conflation of power (managerial relationships) and empowerment (leadership relationships) proves problematic. The more hierarchical the management structures, the more the liberation of leadership capacity is likely to be stifled. This has huge implications for the organizational arrangements of schools. The more the status and worth systems of schools relate to position in hierarchy, the harder it is for distributed leadership to operate. Peter Senge (1990) argues that in learning organizations leaders have to leave their status at the door. Even more problematic, though, in hierarchically conceived structures, is for others to leave the leader's status at the door.

Lateral leadership is equally problematic. For leadership to operate across an organization, opportunities for collaboration between adults of different role and status levels (or even adults and pupils) need naturally to occur across and between what might otherwise be organizationally separate and balkanized cells or units (departments, faculties, phase teams etc). Organizationally, schools find this hard.

So, if leadership cannot readily be delegated down the system (because people have to be empowered), and if opportunities to lead across the system are problematic (because of organizational barriers) then, for leadership to grow, the argument is that 'school as organization' must adapt and reshape its practices in order to generate natural contexts for people to take responsibility in working with and through others. What is needed is the development of new organizational processes such as internal networks, joint workgroups (Peterson and Brietzke 1994), study groups (Marsick and Watkins 1994) or flexible enquiry teams (Louis and Kruse 1995) – what Harris and Lambert call an organizational 'repertoire of continuous learning interactions'.

How might distributed leadership operate in practice?

There is a relationship between leadership and learning. This book argues the interdependence of the two. It views opportunities for collaborative learning as being the core activity for the expansion of leadership capacity, and as the key to developing professional learning communities (see section 3). The key element in the development of leadership 'is the notion of learning together, and the construction of meaning and knowledge collectively and collaboratively. Such leadership allows opportunities to surface and it mediates perceptions, values, beliefs, information and assumptions through continuous conversations' (p. 17).

Similarly, Michael Fullan (1998) offers an insight into the organizational conditions that can give rise to multiple opportunities for leadership when he writes that:

All change is a hypothesis – a process of action, enquiry and experimentation to create a cumulative and collective knowledge about what works and how it works from within. Engaging staff in this process is a means of reculturing. This change to the ways of working – the norms, values and relationships – is a process of restructuring . . . There are no clear solutions. Life is a path you beat while you walk it. It is the walking that beats the path. It is not the path that makes the walk.

Leadership opportunities such as those described – enquiry partnerships, action learning sets and study groups – generate a dialectic within schools. This model of capacity creation, which is knowledge driven, socially cohesive and purposeful, encourages the study of practice and the collaborative generation of ideas. It involves collective meaning-making in the light of emerging knowledge and understandings from enquiry. To use Linda Lambert's word, it is 'constructivist' (Lambert *et al.* 1997). It is where leadership and organizational growth collide, where knowledge-creation and the implementation of change connect; because 'such leadership also creates action that grows out of these new and shared understandings. This transformative dimension (positive and purposeful change) is the core of leadership – and, by definition, it is dispersed or distributed' (Harris and Lambert).

These relationships between collaborative activity, leadership and capacity are not merely theoretical – nor generalizations from 'outlier' case study contexts. They have an empirical base, too. Silins and Mulford (2001) in a major study involving Australian schools concluded that dispersed forms of leadership are characterized by 'shared learning through teams of staff working together to augment the range of knowledge and skills available for the organization to change and anticipate future developments'. They further discovered a positive relationship between such forms of leadership learning and student achievement.

It follows, then, that groups of teachers, working together on collaborative enquiry or planning activity, led by someone whose leadership is not entwined with role status, provides an 'organic' organizational model for the expression and growth of leadership capacity. It also provides the lateral learning impetus required to break down organizational barriers and to foster cultural norms hospitable to internal networks. Knowledge-creation and knowledge-sharing are processes at the heart of the leadership of collaborative enquiry. Capacity generation is the outcome – from both the process and the products.

What is the role of the designated leader?

I argued earlier that leadership is not trait theory – leadership and leader are not the same thing. Harris and Lambert make the case that leadership is about collaborative learning that leads to purposeful change. This learning has direction towards higher aspirations and shared purposes. Yet we have also argued that organizational redesign is a prerequisite for the development of contexts in which such leadership and learning happen naturally. It is the design change that facilitates professional engagement, and that is a tough process to lead, both because external conditions are unpropitious and because internal resistance is almost inevitable.

Everyone has both the potential and the entitlement to contribute towards leadership. The designated leader's role in the scenario described here is partly to facilitate this entitlement. In part this means creating the organizational conditions, the climate and the support for all members to be able to contribute their latent leadership – to release both the kinetic and the potential energy of leadership. This is a subtle challenge. In part, though, it means also having the confidence of vision and the strength of will to operate against both the external and internal grain. It is the second paradox described earlier and the reason why the most advanced sites tend to have extraordinary leaders.

One of the most potent concepts in this book is the assertion that leading is a skilled and complicated undertaking, but one that every member of the school community can learn in a supportive context.

Leadership, after all, is democracy in action. It involves the valuing of the multiple voices that make up the lived experience of school – and in this way will inevitably begin to embrace pupil voices, too. Expressed as such, leadership is a collective endeavour and school change is a shared undertaking. The sustainable improvement journey requires the capacity that shared, inclusive and collaborative activity can bring. Leadership of this order requires the redistribution of power and authority.

Consistent with the changed forms of headteacher action outlined in the above discussion, all of the images in Joseph Murphy's (Murphy *et al*. 1993, adapted) metaphors for modern school leaders have resonance:

- Headteacher as Leader
- School Leader as Moral Agent
- School Leader as Organizational Architect
- School Leader as Social Architect
- School Leader as Educator
- School Leader as Servant
- School Leader as Member of a Community
- School Leadership as Capacity Building.

In organizations where leadership is liberated, available to all, related to collaborative processes and learning, the role of the symbolic leader (the headteacher) is, as Murphy suggests, pivotal, but not superordinate. In moving towards distributed leadership models, the leader is the critical change agent – the guardian and facilitator of transitions. Transition leadership is the new focus for transformation.

Through the liberation of leadership in this way, a premium will also be placed upon alignment and common purpose. Highest order alignment comes from shared values, beliefs and purposes. Designated leaders (headteachers) in such schools will enact and live out the values, both as leader and follower. They will take seriously their own learning – educational, pedagogical and interpersonal. They will be coach and facilitator, social architect and community builder.

Such leaders, then, will design the organizational architecture, they will nurture the social capital that facilitates distributive leadership and collaboration – a social capital built on trust and 'co-dependency'. Trust relationships in turn allow open engagement and knowledge sharing. Such leaders will also unite the school around shared values and higher order purposes. They will be articulate in mobilizing values-identification and alignment and in articulating and re-affirming beliefs. They will 'disseminate eloquence' (Weick 1976) and will hold people accountable to shared value commitments. They will have the moral courage progressively to re-structure their schools around the twin strands of higher order purpose and the values of the school. It follows that in organizations seeking to learn together in this way, school leaders give away power, distribute leadership and support others to be successful.

Such leaders are unusual people and it is an improbable aspiration to ask 24,000 headteachers to do this alone. Or, as Linda Lambert says in Chapter 8, 'We cannot save education one school at a time!'

Small steps forward

In their introduction, Alma Harris and Linda Lambert refer to the potential role of the National College for School Leadership in England. In addition to inheriting and developing three national training programmes, the College has been pursuing an innovative agenda compatible with the vision explored in the pages that follow. Early research on capacity building (Hadfield 2002; Hopkins and Jackson 2002) has been well received, as have the programmes arising from it. The team leadership research conducted by one of the authors of this book has in turn informed the development of the potentially influential 'Leading from the Middle' programme (*www.ncsl.org.uk*). The New Visions for Early Headship programme is designed to develop leaders who understand the relationship between leadership and learning, who value the role of knowledge creation and who appreciate the contribution of constructivism to organizational development.

However, schools are not currently well designed for either capacity creation or distributed leadership. Some are weak on the foundation conditions – turbulent, under strain, driven by conflicting pressures. Others are rendered incoherent by the forces of external change, the reform agenda and the expectations of multiple accountabilities. Some schools are inarticulate about shared values, unclear about the beliefs that unite them. Most (secondary in particular) have structures designed when stability, efficiency and the management of stasis were the expectations. They are unsuited to a context of multiple change and creativity. Distributed leadership, the unifying component of capacity, requires flexible organizations, metabolisms rather than structures, purposeful permutations of teams and collaborations – and widely available opportunities for leadership. Few schools currently function comfortably in that kind of way.

Schools also are not currently structured in ways that facilitate the natural growth of leadership or lateral learning. Predominantly, leadership is locked into management structures. If we are to achieve distributive leadership models, we must therefore re-design the internal social architecture of schools and the external context within which they operate. Such re-design will need to normalize collaborative learning – within and between schools – by which means leadership can be more widely available and unrelated to role status.

In response to this, in 2002 NCSL launched a national initiative entitled Networked Learning Communities. It invited groups of schools (between six and sixteen) to submit collaboratively written proposals to form networks, broadly around the theme of developing interdependent professional learning communities. Each had to commit to proposals within five levels of learning – pupil, adult, leadership, organizational and school-to-school – in turn supported by enquiry processes and a commitment to learning on behalf of one another. The NLCs are intended to provide a context for shared exploration of the ideas presented in this book, based upon two hypotheses. The first is that schools and school leaders need to model the collaborative learning processes beyond their school that they are seeking to develop within it.

The second is that it is easier to build capacity and leadership density together than it is alone.

Distributed leadership also requires shelter from external pressures and accountabilities – and leaders who will deflect, interpret and energize by being opportunistic, optimistic and aspirational in the interpretation of public expectations. Schools can do this better and can be stronger together, rather than alone.

Good theory, and this book is full of it, demands the respect of being put to the test of practice. By this I mean not just seeking to implement the ideas in individual outlier locations – which the case studies in this book illustrate can be achieved – but by seeking to develop models that can begin the process of taking the ideas and aspirations to scale. Networked Learning Communities are seeking to do that, building leadership capacity on an ambitious scale and using school-to-school collaborations to problem-solve some of the challenges, paradoxes and inhibitors outlined in this foreword.

David Jackson
National College for School Leadership (NCSL)

References and Further reading

Argyris, C. (1976) *Increasing Leadership Effectiveness*. New York: Wiley-Interscience.

Firestone,W.A. (1989) Using reform: conceptualizing district initiative, *Educational Evaluation and Policy Analysis*, 11(2): 151–64.

Fullan, M. and Steigelbauer, S. (1991) *The New Meaning of Educational Change*. New York: Teachers College Press.

Fullan, M. (1998) Leadership for the 21st century: breaking the bonds of dependency, *Educational Leadership*, 55(7).

Hadfield, M. (2002) Growing Capacity for School Development, NCSL Research Report.

Hargreaves, D. (2001) A capital theory of school effectiveness and improvement, *British Educational Research Journal*, 27(4).

Harris, A. (2002) Effective leadership in schools facing challenging contexts, *School Leadership and Management*, 22(1): 15–27.

Hopkins, D. and Jackson, D. (2002) Building capacity for leadership and learning. Paper presented at the International Congress for School Effectiveness and Improvement, Copenhagen, January.

Jackson, D. (2000) School improvement and the planned growth of leadership capacity. Paper presented at BERA Conference, Cardiff, September.

Jackson, D. and Southworth, G. (2001) Braiding knowledge for impact metaphor and reality in NCSL's research strategy. Paper presented at the UCEA Conference, Cincinnati, November.

Lambert, L. (1998) *Building Leadership Capacity in Schools*. Alexandria, VA: Association for Supervision and Curriculum Development.

Lambert, L., Kent, K., Richert, A. E., Collay, M. and Dietz, M.E. (1997) *Who Will Save Our Schools? Teachers As Constructivist Leaders*. Thousand Oaks, CA: Corwin Press.

Louis, K.S. & Kruse, S.D. (1995) *Professionalism and Community: Perspectives on Reforming Urban Schools*. Thousand Oaks, CA: Corwin Press.

Marsick, V.J. and Watkins, K.E. (1994) The learning organization: an integrative vision for HRD, *Human Resource Development Quarterly*, 5(4): 353–60.

Meyer, J.W. (1992) Conclusion: institutionalization and the rationality of formal organizational structure, in J.W. Meyer and W.R. Scott (eds.) *Organizational Environments: Ritual and Rationality*. London, New Delhi: Newbury Park.

Miller, R., Michalski, W. and Stevens, B. (1999) *21st Century Technologies: Promises and Perils of a Dynamic Future*.

Mitchell, C. and Sackney, L. (2000) *Profound Improvement: Building Capacity for a Learning Community*. Lisse, NL: Swets & Zeitlinger.

Murphy, J., Beck, L. and Lynn, G. (1993) *Understanding the Principalship: Metaphorical Themes 1920s–1990s*. New York: Teachers College Press.

Peterson, K.D. and Brietzke, R. (1994) *Building Collaborative Cultures: Seeking Ways to Reshape Urban Schools*. Oak Brook, IL: North Central Regional Educational Laboratory.

Senge, P. (1990) *The Fifth Discipline*. New York: Doubleday.

Sergiovanni, T.J. (1994) *Building Community in Schools*. San Francisco: Jossey Bass.

Sergiovanni, T.J. (2001) *Leadership: What's in it for Schools?*, London: Routledge/Falmer.

Silins, H. and Mulford, B. (2001) Reframing schools: the case for system, teacher and student learning. Paper presented at the Eighth International Literacy and Education Research Network Conference on Learning, Spetses, Greece, 4–8 July.

Spears, L. (1995) *Reflections on Leadership*. London: John Wiley & Sons.

Spillane, J., Halverson, R. and Diamond, J. (2001) *Towards a Theory of Leadership Practice: A Distributed Perspective*. Northwestern University, Institute for Policy Research Working Paper.

Weick, K. (1976) Educational organizations as loosely coupled systems, *Administrative Science Quarterly*, 21(1): 1–19.

PREFACE

In 1998, the best selling book by Linda Lambert, *Building Leadership Capacity in Schools*, was published by ASCD. It captured the imagination of educators across the world and generated a renewed interest in leadership development in schools. This book is an adaptation of *Building Leadership Capacity in Schools* and reflects some of the ideas contained in the sequel *Developing Sustainable Leadership Capacity in Schools and LEAs*. It deliberately places key concepts, exemplars and rubrics contained in both books in the context of the English educational system. The central ideas within the book have been retained, along with a focus on practical guidance and directly addressing issues of importance to those working in schools. This is not a theoretical book about leadership, as many such texts already exist. In contrast, this book draws on the practical experience of the authors and their work with schools over many years. Both have worked with schools in an improvement and development capacity in their different contexts and have a wide range of experience of how schools improve.

The main aim of this book is to provide those in schools with an insight into the principles and practice of generating leadership capacity. Its central purpose is to exemplify how capacity building takes place within schools and to illuminate how leadership capacity is at the heart of professional learning communities. Drawing on case study examples, the book highlights the process of capacity building in action. Its core message is that all schools can build leadership capacity irrespective of context, performance or previous history.

The future challenge for all schools will be how to sustain improvement in times of change. Evidence suggests that sustainable school improvement is dependent on schools' ability to generate the internal conditions and to build professional learning communities. Leadership plays a key part in this process and it is hoped that this book will assist leaders at all levels within schools to build the capacity for sustained school improvement.

Alma Harris
Linda Lambert

ACKNOWLEDGEMENTS

We would like to thank ACSD for agreeing to allow the original text of *Building Leadership Capacity in Schools* to be revised and adapted. Without their co-operation this book would not have been possible. We are also grateful to Open University Press for agreeing to publish this book. Particular thanks go to Shona Mullen, commissioning editor at Open University Press for her enthusiasm and support for this project. Thanks also to David Jackson for writing such an illuminating and thought-provoking foreword.

Linda acknowledges and thanks two special friends: Alma Harris for having the great idea to write this book and taking on most of the responsibility for doing so, and Rosemary Forster, University of Alberta, for introducing us.

Alma offers a personal acknowledgement to Sarah Mary Williams (1969–2002) – your wisdom was beyond your years.

Finally, we would both like to acknowledge and thank

all the teachers who have helped us write this book. Their experiences, feelings and insights about the process of building leadership capacity for school improvement are captured and reflected in the pages that follow.

INTRODUCTION

> There are many leaders, not just one. Leadership is distributed. It resides not solely in the individual at the top, but in every person at every level who in one way or another, acts as a leader.
>
> (Goleman 2002: 14)

Good leaders captivate, enthuse and inspire us. We all know good leadership when we see it, like good schools or good teaching it is relatively easy to identify and describe. Good leaders have integrity, charisma, strong values, emotional intelligence and moral purpose. They have energy, drive and enthusiasm. They motivate us and challenge us and remain optimistic even in the face of adversity. They exist at all levels in any organization and most importantly, they generate development, change and improvement. It is for this reason that there are thousands of books written every year on the subject of leadership, hundreds of courses run and dozens of new programmes devoted to perfecting leadership styles and qualities. But does this level of investment pay dividends? Are our schools transformed through improved or effective leadership?

In the current educational climate, the answer to both questions is quite firmly in the affirmative. A 'new wave' of interest in school leadership has been prompted by a general concern about improving standards in schools and raising levels of student achievement. On the crest of this 'new wave' is the National College for School Leadership. Its research and development work has opened up a challenging debate about the nature, location and quality of leadership practices in schools. Since its launch, the National College for School Leadership (NCSL) has been active in developing new leadership programmes and in pursuing an innovative research agenda of practical utility for school leaders. However, in England as in other countries, the real driving force behind the renewed emphasis on leadership has been the desire to raise standards of educational achievement and performance.

The 'standards-stampede' is a familiar part of the discourse of educational change across the globe. Within this discourse, leadership features predominantly as a means to generating and mobilizing change across systems and within schools. There is a general expectation and a strong consensus about the potential of school leaders to contribute to improved educational performance and achievement. The research findings from diverse countries draw very similar conclusions about the centrality of leadership in school improvement. Schools that are improving have leaders who make a significant and measurable contribution to the development of the school and the teachers. The potential of leadership to influence school improvement remains uncontested but the type of leadership required for sustainable school improvement remains a matter of debate.

The volume of literature devoted to leadership offers little clarity on the simple but profound question 'What type of leadership generates and sustains school improvement?' The various positions taken by writers and researchers on the subject is often contradictory and frequently convoluted. Much of the work is overly theoretical offering those in schools a complex and rather inaccessible picture of effective school leadership in action. It is difficult to see how 'transformational', 'moral', 'learning-centred', 'instructional' and 'pedagogical' leadership relate and it is even more difficult to see how those in schools translate this amalgam of theory into any practical guidance. At the other end of the spectrum are the reductionist, 'self-help' leadership books that offer simplistic, de-contextualized guides to leading a team, a group or a school. While they may be worth a minute or two at a motorway service station, they offer little guidance for those who are serious about improving their schools.

Alternatively, if you do find yourself browsing in the education section of your local bookstore, pick at random one or two books on the theme of educational leadership. You will soon see that for 'leadership' read 'headship' or, at best, the 'senior management team'. Leadership in schools still tends to equate with position, or authority, you have to be a recognized leader within the organization. Ironically, while those in industry and business have understood for well over a decade the limitations of the 'chief executive' approach to leadership, we in education still believe in the leadership abilities of those at the top to change, develop and improve a school. This is not to suggest that the head is now redundant or that the senior management team should be disbanded, rather it is to argue that their leadership is necessary but not sufficient for sustained school improvement. Research shows that the most effective heads generate the capacity for improvement through investing in the development of others, by distributing leadership within the organization and developing the systems that invite skilful involvement. In short, they 'build the capacity' for school improvement by empowering others to lead and to develop the school (Hadfield and Chapman 2002).

Capacity building?

But what exactly is meant by 'capacity building' and how is this achieved within schools? From a relatively simple perspective, capacity building is concerned with providing opportunities for people to work together in a new way. Collegial relations are therefore at the core of capacity building. One of the distinguishing features of schools that are failing is the sheer absence of any professional community, discourse and trust. Within improving schools, a climate of collaboration exists and there is a collective commitment to work together. This climate is not simply given but is the deliberate result of discussion, development and dialogue among those working within the organization. An improving school community con-sists of teachers who are active in constructing meaning and collaborating in mutual enquiry and learning. An improving school is also a learning community where the learning of teachers receives the same attention as the learning of pupils. Relationships are therefore critically important in the school improvement endeavour. As Microsoft endorses in its mission statement, 'people are our greatest asset'.

Building capacity essentially involves building relation-ships, building trust and building community. But devel-opment of individuals is not enough. Capacity building is about ensuring that the school is a 'self-developing force' (Senge 1990) through investing in those school and class-room level conditions that promote development and change (Hopkins and Harris 2001). The limitations of 'top-down' and 'bottom-up' change are well documented. Both fail to recognize that unless the internal conditions within a school are pre-disposed to change and development, irrespective of how 'good' the new initiative or change is, it will inevitably flounder. Unless schools have built the internal capacity to manage change and sustain improve-ment, well-intentioned reform will continue to have little impact. The 'conveyor belt' of change keeps initiatives, rather than schools, moving.

What does capacity building look and feel like in practice? Hopkins and Jackson (2002) point us towards some useful central concepts and perspectives that offer an operational definition of capacity. The first is the central importance of the *people* – the leaders, educational professionals and students – and the expansion of their contributions. A second relates to the alignment and synergies created when internal arrangements, connections and *teams* are working optimally. A third corresponds to the organizational arrangements (the 'programme coherence' and the 'internal networks') that support *personal* and *interpersonal* capacity development. The fourth is more subtle, but crucially important. It is the territory of shared values, social cohesion, *trust*, well-being, moral purpose, involvement, care, valuing and being valued, which is the operational field of 'leadership'. The two key components of a capacity building model are the professional learning community (the people, interpersonal and organizational arrangements working in developmental or learning synergy) and the leadership capacity (as the route to generating the social cohesion and trust to make this happen).

In this sense, capacity building is concerned with developing the conditions, skills and abilities to manage and facilitate productive change at school level. It also necessitates a particular form of leadership to generate school improvement, change and development. While the 'superhero' model of leadership may seem beguilingly attractive, evidence suggests that this approach to leadership is unlikely to generate the internal conditions for sustainable school self-renewal and growth. For this to be achieved a new form of leadership is required, one that focuses on learning, both organizational and individual, and one that invests in a community of learning – parents, teachers, pupils and governors.

Since the early 1990s a considerable amount of attention has been given to the notion of the school as a 'learning community'. It has been suggested that 'developing a community of practice may be the single best most important way to improve a school' (Sergiovanni 2000: 139). In a learning community emphasis is placed on the personal growth and development of individuals as a means of generating improved learning outcomes. In contrast, in a learning community there is a central commitment to building the capacity to learn – this is the end product, 'a living community that learns' (Mitchell and Sackney 2000). For schools the implications are very clear. If schools are to sustain improvement over time, they will need to ensure that they are communities of learning. But how do schools become communities of learning? How do they generate the conditions where learning can flourish and grow?

Unfortunately, 'community' has come to mean any gathering of people in a school or social setting. But building a 'learning community' asks more of us than just simply gathering together. It assumes a focus on mutual regard, caring and integrity. It requires shared purpose and the creation of an environment where pupils and teachers learn together. The development of such a community depends on three important and interrelated components. First, trust among those who are working together; second, knowledge of what the issues or tasks are that need to be addressed to move the school forwards; and third, the leadership capacity to undertake the necessary work in a way that allows modification and encourages reflection.

This book

This book is essentially about building leadership capacity to create learning communities. It is premised on the notion that if schools are to improve and to sustain improvement they can no longer be reliant on the leadership capabilities of just one person. The term 'leadership capacity' in this book means 'broad-based skilful involvement in the work of leadership' (Lambert 1998: 5). This includes teachers, parents and pupils in the work of leadership but in a focused, skilful and purposeful way.

Leadership capacity refers to the capacity of an organization to lead itself and to sustain that effort when key individuals leave. It is primarily concerned with creating the
conditions within schools for self-renewal and growth.

The major challenge facing schools in the twenty-first
century is not how to improve but how to sustain
improvement in rapidly changing times. In the late 1970s,
the great American educator Ron Edmonds suggested
that we know all we need to know to improve our schools.
Enough is known already about effective school improvement (Hopkins 2001). The international research
base is rich and the empirical evidence consistent in high-
lighting school improvement interventions and processes
that work (Harris and Crispeels forthcoming). The burn-
ing issue is not how to improve schools but how to sustain
improvement in the face of increased globalization and
rapid technological advance.

In the current climate, the ability of school leaders to
make a difference depends on their interpretation of and
responses to the tensions, constraints, demands and
choices that they face. Effective leaders must know how
to promote information and to generate knowledge creation and sharing within the organization. At the same
time they will need to create opportunities for others to
lead and to take responsibility for innovation and change.
Those schools that have built the capacity to manage
change and have instigated processes that will assist them
to learn and in some cases to 'unlearn' will be those that
will continue to flourish and grow. The central leadership
task is therefore to generate the conditions and create the
climate for improvement to be initiated and sustained.
This implies a form of leadership that is distributed and
shared, that belongs to the many rather than the few.

This book considers some of the leadership processes
that contribute to building the capacity for change and
improvement. It does not claim to be the definitive or last
word on leadership but offers those who are interested or
engaged in school improvement some practical ways of
generating leadership capacity. It takes the perspective

that leadership is a fluid and emergent entity rather than a fixed phenomenon. It implies a different power relationship within the school where the distinctions between followers and leaders blur. It also opens up the possibility for all teachers to become leaders at various times and suggests that leadership is a shared and collective endeavour that can engage all teachers irrespective of age or experience. The overarching message about effective leadership for school improvement is one of building the community of the school in its widest sense, that is through developing and involving others.

Leadership is therefore a critical and essential variable in the process of generating capacity for school improvement. The prime purpose of leadership is to build the capacity for individuals to flourish, for schools to continually improve and change and for young people to be the best they can be. It is leadership that is people-centred and premised on core personal and professional values. It is this form of leadership that is at the heart of school improvement and provides the central theme of this book.

PART 1

BUILDING LEADERSHIP

CAPACITY

1 WHAT IS LEADERSHIP

CAPACITY?

> Good leaders foster good leadership at other levels.
> Leadership at other levels produces a steady stream of
> future leaders for the system as a whole.
>
> (Fullan 2001: 10)

When Jennifer Fielding decided to apply for a job at
Rookwood Comprehensive School, it was with good reason. With almost three years of teaching experience, she
was beginning to feel a new sense of confidence. Not that
she knew all there was to know about teaching but she
was ready to be more involved in work beyond the
classroom. She found herself more concerned with children in other classrooms, families in the surrounding
community and felt uncomfortable with the restrictions
of her subject area.

That year, she had participated in several LEA courses
and had been part of a National College of School Leadership (NCSL) networked learning community project
involving ten schools. There she had met a few teachers

from Rookwood Comprehensive School. She was impressed. They talked with clear excitement about what was going on at Rookwood; they seemed to share an enthusiasm about the improvement work they were trying to accomplish. By mid-April, she had made her decision. When the head of English post was advertised, she applied and was successful.

In early September she was immersed in getting ready for and beginning to teach in her new job at Rookwood. She was given a school mentor, Gary, who had taught at the school for eight years. The orientation and support were extremely helpful. Gary shared lesson plans, answered questions, and introduced her to other teachers, and a few active parents. Yet in the corridors and staff room she detected a familiar tone: cynicism, misplaced humour, even anger about the school's future plans for improvement. 'What happened?' Jennifer asked. 'This isn't quite what I expected.' Gary replied, 'You see, our head left.'

This is not an unfamiliar story. In many schools throughout the country: momentum, energy and growing commitment begin to form around some key improvement ideas and a change among key personnel or mandated directions derails the effort. Even the most committed teachers become discouraged and cynical as improvement efforts diminish when the head leaves. How far will teachers go on the conveyor belt of change only to be told to get off and start again?

Ask any number of strong and seemingly effective heads what happened in the school that they just left. Many will reluctantly admit that the failure of succession planning and over-reliance on their leadership meant the school was once again reverting to previous practices and disbanding from school improvement efforts. However, schools and people never entirely return to the way they were before. Each time they rebound from a failed or terminated effort, they are more deeply disappointed, more cynical, more wounded. Each time, improvement in that school becomes more difficult to achieve. As long as improvement is dependent on a single person or a few people or outside directions and forces, it will fail. Schools, and the people in them, have a propensity to depend too much on a strong head or other authority figures for direction and guidance.

Any number of responses could now occur at Rookwood Comprehensive School. A few key teachers could refuse to let their progress slip away and decide to take hold of the reins of reform and pull things back together. The new head could be strong and wise and able to work with the school to recapture some of its previous momentum. The school could choose to envelop itself with regrets and remorse and let go of cherished innovations. When Jennifer asked her powerful question, 'What happened?' several teachers at Rookwood Comprehensive School were enmeshed in a stage of self-pity. Those who had been tentative about the reforms were quick to point out how fragile they were; those who had been somewhat resistant felt vindicated. Hadn't they warned the head that the school was moving too fast, with too many changes? Accustomed to looking to someone with formal authority to lead the way, the teacher analysts failed to recognize that leadership lies within the school not just with the head. They were unable to see that sustained school improvement requires a school to build its own leadership capacity if it is to stay afloat, to assume internal responsibility for reform, and to maintain a momentum for self-renewal. But how is this achieved in practice? How is leadership capacity generated and sustained?

Building leadership capacity *means broad-based, skilful involvement in the work of leadership*. At least two critical conditions would have been necessary in order to establish enduring leadership capacity at Rookwood:

1 There would need to be a significant number of skilful *teacher leaders* who understood the shared vision in the school, the full scope of the work underway, and were able to carry it out. These teachers ideally would be

involved with the selection and induction of the new head.

2 There would need to be commitment to the central work of *self-renewing* schools. This work involves reflection, enquiry, conversations and focused action – professional behaviours that are an integral part of daily work.

These conditions speak to two critical dimensions that this book will explore in depth: (1) breadth of involvement and (2) understandings and skilfulness of those involved.

Understandings and skilfulness involve more than the knowledge of an innovation (that is, new teaching approaches, material or arrangements). The skilfulness addressed here refers to those skills of *leadership* that allow other teachers to capture the imagination of their colleagues, enable them to negotiate real changes in their own schools and to tackle the inevitable conflicts that arise from such courageous undertakings. This book explores in detail the meaning and strategies involved in building leadership capacity for school improvement. Before focusing on the concept of 'leadership capacity' it is important to say a little more about what we mean by 'school improvement ' and 'leadership'.

School improvement

For school improvement to occur, there has to be a commitment to changing 'the way we do things around here' for the better. School improvement is essentially a process of changing school culture. To achieve this, teachers need to be committed to a process of change that involves them in examining and changing their own practice. Research has demonstrated the vital importance of teacher development in school level change. It has consistently shown that teacher development is inextricably linked to school development and is an essential part of school improvement. It has shown that within improving schools leadership is shared and distributed. Also, school improvement work has highlighted the importance of teacher collaboration. A school culture that promotes collegiality, trust, collaborative working relationships and that focuses on teaching and learning is more likely to be self-renewing and responsive to improvement efforts.

In addition, the evidence reinforces the importance of teacher enquiry and reflection. The analysis and application of research findings by teachers as part of their routine professional activity has been shown to have had a positive effect on the quality of teaching and learning. There is evidence from highly successful school improvement projects to show that providing teachers with the opportunity to enquire about their practice leads to changed attitudes, beliefs and behaviours. Moreover, these changes in attitudes, beliefs and behaviours positively affect their classroom teaching and result in improved learning outcomes for pupils. School improvement depends on sustaining a culture of opportunity for pupils and teachers. This depends on teachers and pupils who trust one another and work together with a common purpose. It depends on building a school community that is inclusive and values, above all, individual development and achievement.

In short, effective school leaders build the capacity for improvement within their schools. They generate the conditions and create the climate for improvement to be initiated and sustained. Effective leaders orchestrate rather than dictate improvement and create learning communities within their schools. The role of leadership in school improvement is primarily to act as a catalyst in creating a learning environment for both teachers and pupils. This necessarily involves building the capacity within the school for learning and improvement to take place. Schools that 'build the capacity' for implementing change are more likely to sustain improvement over time. In other words, they are able to generate both the readiness to change and the internal capacity to manage the change process.

At the core of successful school improvement is a form of contructivist leadership (Lambert *et al.* 1998). It is a form of leadership that is about learning together and constructing meaning and knowledge collectively and collaboratively. This approach to leadership creates the opportunities to surface and mediate perceptions; to enquire about and generate ideas together; to seek to reflect on and make sense of work in the light of shared beliefs and new information; and to create actions that grow out of these new understandings. Such is the core of leadership. Leadership is about learning together.

Leadership

Most of us probably think of a particular person and associated set of behaviours when we think of 'leadership'. When we use the word 'leadership', the next sentence often suggests what the head did or did not do of importance. 'We have strong leadership in the school.' 'We have weak leadership in this school, and we are clearly not going to achieve our goals.' 'We need a change of leadership!' Most often these assertions refers to the head. Leadership is generally considered to be synonymous with a person in a position of formal authority.

When we equate the powerful concept of 'leadership' with the behaviours of one person, we are limiting the achievement of broad-based participation on the part of a community or society. School leadership needs to be a broad concept that is separated from person, role and a discrete set of individual behaviours. It needs to be embedded in the school community as a whole. Such a broadening of the concept of leadership suggests shared responsibility for a shared purpose of community.

When we equate 'leadership' with 'leader', we are immersed in 'trait theory': if only a leader possessed these certain traits, we would have good leadership. This tendency has caused those who might have rolled up their sleeves and pitched in to help, to abstain from the work of leadership, thereby abdicating both responsibilities and their opportunities. While leaders do perform acts of leadership, a separation of the concepts can allow us to reconceptualize leadership itself.

Leadership needs to speak to a group broader than the individual leader. This breadth can become more evident if we consider the connections or learning processes among individuals in a school community. This concept, which Lambert (1998) calls 'leadership', is broader than the sum total of its 'leaders' for it also involves an energy flow or synergy generated by those who choose to lead. Sometimes we think of our reactions to an energized environment as being caught up in the excitement and stimulation of an idea or a movement. It is this wave of energy and purpose that engages and pulls others into the work of leadership. This is a group of 'leaders', engaged in improving a school.

The key notion in this definition of leadership is that leadership is about learning together and constructing meaning and knowledge collectively and collaboratively. It involves opportunities to surface and mediate percep-tions, values, beliefs, information and assumptions through continuing conversations. It means generating ideas together; to seek to reflect on and make sense of work in the light of shared beliefs and new information; and to create actions that grow out of these new under-standings. Such is the core of leadership. Leadership is about learning together.

When the Rookwood Comprehensive School staff and community, working together, identified and clarified their values, beliefs, assumptions and perceptions about what they wanted children to know and be able to do, an important next step was to discover which of these values and expectations were now being achieved. Such a dis-covery required that the staff and community members enquire about their own practice. What information do we have? What information do we need? The problems to be solved rested in the discrepancies: is there a gap between our current practice and achievements and what we want children to be able to know and do?

These conversations clarified and framed the school's plans and actions for improvement. Further, these conversations also identified responsibilities and strategies for implementation and continuous feedback that the whole school community understood, not just the head or the head and one or two teachers. This is a difficult undertaking. Throughout this book, we describe the leadership dispositions, understandings and skills that are essential if schools are to tackle such elegant and demanding work.

Using the Rookwood example above, let's look more closely at the *key reciprocal learning processes* that engaged this school in the process of self-renewal. In chapters 3–5, the case studies describe some of the ways in which these processes are carried out in schools.

1 *Surface, clarify and define values, beliefs, assumptions, perceptions and experiences.* Rookwood chose to use this process as a means to discover what they valued about pupils' learning (what pupils should know and be able to do). Such an effort requires many small and informal conversations as well as large-group work, in which teachers confront what they already believe, think and know about the school. Fundamentally, learning is about altering these personal schemas and shared beliefs as new purposes are created and evolve.

2 *Enquire into practice.* School improvement necessitates enquiring into practice. It means examining or generating information (data) that could point to whether or not – and how well – pupils are learning. These data include pupil work and disaggregated performance and attendance data. Teachers must be involved in identifying and securing these data if they are to use what they find to generate priorities for improvement.

3 *Construct meaning and knowledge.* In order to improve, a school must decide on strategies that fit the particular issue or problem that the school currently faces. In this

sense the school must adopt a differentiated approach to change that pays attention to the particular context of the school and the specific challenges it is facing. In this respect, school development and improvement needs to be 'custom built' to match the needs of each individual school. The limitations of the 'one size fits all' approach to improvement are well documented and well known.

4 *Frame action and develop implementation plans.* In order to sustain improvement there has to be a means of implementing plans and evaluating progress. The drive for improvement is important if momentum is not to be lost or energy dissipated. Early signs of success are important as is the presence of feedback systems that remind teachers of the progress and gains being made.

These processes are part of a repertoire of continuous learning interactions. Teachers need to continually tie their work conversations to their shared purpose: 'Now, what is it that we are trying to do here?' 'Why is that?' Altering personal and collective understandings requires revisiting and reinterpreting ideas many times – in staff rooms, informal small-group dialogue, as well as departmental meetings.

For school improvement to take place, organizational and individual learning must be embedded in a trusting environment in which relationships form a safety net of mutual support and challenge. Especially in the beginning, people are taking risks. Because these processes occur among participants in a school community it means that people are in relationships with one another. To be in authentic relationships with one another means that we provide long-term support for one another, challenging each other to improve and to question our current perceptions, and to learn together. Attention to relationships is therefore critical for, just as in the classroom, 'process is content'.

As Michael Fullan has argued in his work, it is not simply the case that change equates with improvement. Similarly, not all learning processes constitute leadership.

Leadership processes must enable participants to engage in a shared sense of purpose, a purpose made real by the collaboration of committed adults. Leadership has direction, momentum, and it negotiates tough passages. It is this type of leadership we are seeking to 'build the capacity' of to collectively generate purposeful action that allows a school community to keep moving in the face of external demands, imposed change or when an excellent teacher, a charismatic head or a powerful parent leaves.

Summary and key assumptions

1 *Leadership is not trait theory*; leadership and leader are not the same. Leadership can mean (and does mean in this context) the reciprocal learning processes that enable participants to construct and negotiate meanings leading to a shared purpose of schooling.
2 *Leadership is about learning that leads to constructive change*. Learning is among participants and therefore occurs collectively. Learning has direction towards a shared purpose.
3 *Everyone has the potential and right to work as a leader*. Leading is skilled and complicated work that can be learned by every member of the school community. Democracy clearly defines the rights of individuals to actively participate in the decisions that affect their lives.
4 *Leading is a shared endeavour*, the foundation for the democratization of schools. School change is a collective endeavour, therefore, people do this most effectively in the presence of others. The learning journey must be shared; otherwise, shared purpose and action are never achieved.
5 *Leadership requires the redistribution of power and authority*. Shared learning, purpose, action and responsibility demand the realignment of power and authority. LEAs and heads need to explicitly release authority, and teachers need to learn how to enhance

personal power and informal authority (for a fuller examination of this notion, see Lambert *et al.* 1997: 122–43).

These five assumptions form the *conceptual framework* for leadership capacity building for school improvement. Together, they advance the ideas that are essential if we are to develop sustainable, self-renewing and improving schools.

In the next chapter the notion of capacity building is discussed by examining schools with low, moderate and high leadership capacity. The five critical features of schools with high leadership capacity are discussed and ways of building leadership capacity are outlined. In Chapter 3 the role of the head in building leadership capacity is explored. In Chapters 4–6, case studies of schools with differing capacity for improvement are described. The five critical features of schools with high leadership capacity serve as the framework for discussion. Chapter 7 details how to get started on the path to building high leadership capacities. Chapter 8 outlines the role of the LEA, as an external agent in capacity building and Chapter 9 considers how professional development contributes to building leadership capacity. Chapter 10 presents some questions and answers you might have while reading this book. In the Appendix a range of support material is offered to provide you with some of the tools needed to undertake this work.

Before moving on to the next chapter, take some time to reflect upon the following questions:

- What does leadership practice currently look like in your school?
- How far is leadership shared with teachers, pupils and parents?
- To what extent is your school a learning community?
- How could leadership capacity be built in your school?

2 CAPACITY BUILDING

CONNECTS WITH

LEADERSHIP

> A community is like a ship; everyone ought to be pre-
> pared to take the helm.
>
> (Henrik Ibsen)

When the head left Rookwood Comprehensive School, the
school lacked the capacity to sustain its efforts at renewal.
The gap left by her leaving was too large and too
strategically placed (many of the things that she did were
done only by her). The walls came tumbling down – at
least, so it seemed. The reforms that had begun at Rookwood had created a good foundation for further capacity
building: teachers were working together, decisions were
being made jointly, a shared vision was emerging – certainly enough for teachers from other schools to notice.
However, now Rookwood finds itself at a crossroads, one
that is so fragile that those who were unsure are wavering.
Now would be the time for teachers and the new head to

recall their accomplishments and push forward, to use their leadership skills to further the capacity of the school for self-responsibility – this time with broader-based engagement.

Over the past 20 years, 'capacity building' has consistently appeared in the international reform literature, although more in the 1970s and 1990s than in the 1980s. It was a very popular term during the 1970s and referred to creating the experiences and opportunities for people to learn how to do certain things. In the early 1970s, improving schools through capacity building meant that heads would organize the school for improvement, teachers would learn to work in teams, and teachers would talk publicly about what they were doing. The driving force here, although not stated explicitly, is the expansion or thickening of leadership.

In the reform climate in England since the early 1990s, capacity building has taken on new and more urgent importance. Many of the top-down, externally mandated reform strategies have failed to sustain improvement once initial enthusiasm or funding has been removed. In December 2001, the early gains achieved by the National Literacy Strategy suddenly reached a plateau. Like so many other externally driven improvement initiatives year-on-year improvement is hard to sustain, unless the internal capacity exists within schools to sustain it. In essence, many large-scale reform initiatives have focused on the wrong variables – looking at systems rather than classrooms, emphasizing accountability rather than promoting development. They have failed to recognize that without investing substantially in capacity building in schools through teacher enquiry, shared leadership, collaboration and collective responsibility, the potential for sustained school improvement is inevitably diminished.

While there are no blueprints for successful school improvement there are some core activities that have been shown to lead to cultural change. Some of behaviours used to strengthen the school culture include reinforcing with teachers, norms of excellence for their own work, assisting teachers to clarify shared beliefs and values and to act in accord with such beliefs and values. These behaviours have been shown to encourage teacher collaboration, to increase teacher motivation and to improve teachers' self-efficacy. There is evidence to demonstrate a positive relationship between such approaches and school improvement. Culture building includes behaviours aimed at developing school norms, values, beliefs and assumptions that are pupil centred and support continuing professional development. In summary the goal of school improvement is to bring about positive cultural change by altering the processes that occur within the school. For long-term, sustained school improvement to occur, there has to be deep-rooted change inside the school.

Building capacity necessitates building an infrastructure of support that is aligned with the work of the school. This infrastructure involves the philosophy and mission of a school, the selection of personnel, resources (time, money and talent), teacher training, work structures, policies and available outside networks. If an LEA supports the internal capacity building of a school, it would work with the school to develop and establish networks both locally and nationally. Chapter 7 will describe how LEAs might offer schools support for capacity building in more detail.

As noted in Chapter 1, leadership capacity building can be defined as broad-based, skilful involvement in the work of leadership. This perspective requires us to look to two critical dimensions of involvement – breadth and skilfulness:

1 *Broad-based involvement* – involving many people in the work of leadership. This involves headteachers, teachers, parents, pupils, community members, LEA personnel, universities.
2 *Skilful involvement* – a comprehensive understanding and demonstrated proficiency by participants of leadership dispositions, knowledge and skills.

The intersection of these two dimensions creates a dynamic relationship that allows us to describe conditions in schools with different levels of leadership capacity (see Figure 2.1).

Level of involvement

LOW INVOLVEMENT **Quadrant 1 – Stuck school** • Head is autocratic • Co-dependent relationships • Norms of compliance • Lack of innovation • Pupil achievement is poor **LOW SKILLS**	**HIGH INVOLVEMENT** **Quadrant Two – Fragmented school** • Head is laissez-faire • Undefined roles and responsibilities • Norms of individualism • Erratic innovation • Pupil achievement static overall (unless data are disaggregated) **LOW SKILLS**
LOW INVOLVEMENT **Quadrant 3 – Moving school** • Head and key teachers as purposeful leadership team • Polarized staff – pockets of resistance • Norms of reflection and teaching excellence • Effective innovation • Pupil achievement shows slight improvement **HIGH SKILLS**	**HIGH INVOLVEMENT** **Quadrant 4 – Improving school** • Head, teachers, as well as pupils as skilful leaders • Shared vision • Norms of collaboration and collective responsibility • Reflective practice consistently leads to innovation • Pupil achievement is high or improving steadily **HIGH SKILLS**

Figure 2.1 Leadership capacity matrix.

As you consider the matrix, notice that the horizontal axis refers to *breadth of involvement* and the vertical axis refers to *skilfulness*. As these two axes intersect, they create four sets of descriptors that characterize schools with different levels of leadership capacity and offer a cultural typology of four schools. Each set of descriptors gives attention to the role of the formal leader(s), the flow of information, defined teachers roles, relationships among teachers, norms, innovation in teaching and learning, and pupil achievement.

A caveat is necessary here. Whenever complex issues or conditions are divided into neat boxes, it creates a problem. Conditions are never neatly bound or clearly delineated. As you examine this matrix, keep that caveat in mind, realizing that these are approximations that often overlap and intermingle. Below are examples of school 'types' that approximate into each quadrant.

Quadrant 1: 'Stuck school' – low involvement, low skilfulness

A quadrant 1 school is the visibly 'failing school' which is low on involvement and low on skilfulness. (This typology is based upon the work of Hargreaves (1995), Hopkins (1996) and Stoll (1998).) These types of schools are poor at the day-to-day management tasks and tend to be reactive rather than proactive in their approach to deadlines or problem solving. The lack of leadership in such schools means that the necessary organization and planning is not in place. In addition, the culture of fragmentation evident in these schools means that development work is impossible as the fundamental infrastructure necessary to support such development is not secure. These schools are not collegiate and do not have clearly articulated goals, plans and vision.

In such schools the head often exercises *autocratic leadership*. The flow of information is one-way – from the head to the teachers – and there is a large amount of delegation and blaming. Relationships are co-dependent; that is, teachers depend on the head for answers and guidance and the head depends on the teachers to validate and reinforce his or her autocratic style. Those teachers who would be actively resistant in a more open environment express their resistance through silent, nearly invisible ways (that as, leaving as soon as school is out, absenteeism, doctor appointments on INSET days).

There is little innovation in teaching and learning among teachers. Proposals for new practices, to which compliance is expected, come from the top. Where innovation does occur there are short-term improvements in pupil achievement. However, this is not sustainable and quickly returns to where it was before. Consequently, teachers become more disillusioned and disappointed than ever before.

Quadrant 2: 'Fragmented school' – high involvement, low skilfulness

A quadrant 2 school is one that, on the face of it, appears to be coping. It is less tightly managed and controlled than a quadrant 1 school. Those in formal leadership positions may operate much of the time in a laissez-faire and unpredictable fashion (with intermittent periods of autocratic rule). Information, like programmes and relationships, is fragmented, lacking any coherent pattern in the school. For instance, since there are no agreed-on assessment policies, some subjects are failing to adequately assess pupil learning. And since there is no school-wide focus on teaching and learning, poor teaching sometimes goes unnoticed.

These types of schools neglect developmental work. These schools are not obviously failing as they appear to be efficiently run. However, their reluctance to develop or to take on new ideas means that they will at best, remain where they are and at worse, gradually deteriorate. Without an investment in their development such schools will be unlikely to improve. They have the potential to make an enormous contribution to pupil performance and achievement but need to unlock this potential by investing in re-skilling and change.

In such schools there is often a strong ethos of *rugged individualism*, with a few skilled entrepreneurs leading pockets of innovation, and many other participants 'doing their own thing'. Roles and responsibilities are unclear. While overall pupil achievement is static, when data are disaggregated, a few pupils (usually along socio-economic and gender lines) are doing very well while others are doing poorly. This 'achievement-gap', while hidden, has significant implications for schools and for performance levels generally. It points to serious and persistent inequities within the education system that go beyond the influence of my one school.

Quadrant 3: 'Moving school' – high skilfulness, low involvement

A quadrant 3 school may be making progress towards reforms. Such schools tend to approach innovation with great enthusiasm and are viewed by those outside the school in a highly positive way. These schools tend to be viewed by the external world as lively and exciting. These schools like to see themselves as '*go ahead*' but often drive forward innovation at the expense of involvement. On the surface such schools might be mistaken as moving because of their high level of involvement in change and innovation. But the opportunity cost of high levels of development is the neglect of basic maintenance activities.

Moving schools can also be places where fragmentation operates underneath the surface and where innovation overload is a real possibility. They have selected a small leadership team who, along with the head, are gaining some powerful leadership skills. They have learned to use available data to make school decisions. However, only a few key teacher activists have become involved. Pockets of active resistance are strong and increasingly vocal. Those teachers who find themselves in the lonely middle, lack the skills to negotiate their ideas and work through stages of conflict with reluctant teachers. Roles and responsibilities are unclear for those who are not among the designated leaders. There are pockets of strong innovation and excellent classrooms, but focus on pupil learning is not a school-wide norm. Although pupil achievement is showing slight gains, the long-term pattern is similar to that found in quadrant 2.

Quadrant 4: 'Improving school' – high skilfulness, high involvement

A quandrant 4 school is initially a 'professional learning community' involved in self-regulated change. Studies of improving schools have shown that they are highly skilled at generating internal change. Such schools are actively involved in the process of self-renewal but select areas for development and change very carefully. Professional learning communities do not simply respond in a 'knee-jerk' way to external demands but use external change for their own internal improvement purposes. They provide opportunities for teachers to work together but create a balance between internally generated and externally imposed change. They are schools where there is a continual drive for improvement and where teachers are involved in change and development. There is a feeling of energy and enthusiasm within these schools but a real danger of 'burn out' as levels of activity may be too high.

An improving school has high leadership capacity and a head capable of collaboration and inclusive leading. They are schools where teachers have gained the leadership skills necessary to affect the norms, roles and responsibilities of the school. They are schools where the school-wide focus is on both pupil and adult learning, and where decision making is shared. Roles and responsibilities are overlapping, each person taking personal and collective responsibility for the work of leadership. Teachers describe themselves as being part of a *professional community*. Pupil achievement is steadily improving. Even when data are disaggregated, there is relatively little difference among socio-economic or gender groups.

These four quadrants provide very different types of schools and very different scenarios of leadership capacity in schools. There are, of course, numerous other possible scenarios that would blend many of these features in different combinations. In Appendix A, you will find an assessment form for estimating the level of leadership capacity in your school.

Just take a moment to reflect on the following questions:

- Where would you place your school on the leadership capacity matrix?
- What does this say about leadership capacity at your school?
- What needs to be done to move your school or secure your school in quadrant 4 of the matrix?

Critical features of high leadership capacity

The work described in quadrant 4 above is difficult. It needs to be informed and guided by skilled professionals who hold a firm vision of what it means to develop a school with high leadership capacity. This work can be distilled down to the elements in the matrix and the following five critical features of a successful school improvement.

1 Broad-based, skilful involvement in the work of leadership
2 Enquiry-based use of information to inform shared decisions and practice
3 Roles and responsibilities that reflect broad involvement and collaboration

4 Reflective practice and innovation as the norm
5 High or steadily improving pupil achievement.

Below is a description of each critical feature and the leadership dispositions, knowledge and skills essential to the development of such a school.

Broad-based, skilful involvement in the work of leadership
This feature is the essence of leadership capacity and requires attention to two areas: structures and processes for involvement and opportunities to become skilful participants (the two axes on Figure 2.1). A school needs several kinds of working groups. It needs governance groups that are representative of the school's many constituents: teachers, administrators, pupils, parents, community members and, if possible, LEA office personnel and university advisers. Almost as important are the multiple groups needed for getting the work of the school done. These might include collaborative action research groups (ad hoc groups in which all teachers serve at least once), subject level and interdisciplinary teams. As stated in the previous chapter, collaborative work needs to be directly linked to school improvement and pupil learning. Yet the work must be spread out and shared, so that teachers are not overwhelmed with tasks. It is important to note here that there are two kinds of work associated with teacher leadership:

1 taking on different roles and tasks
2 working differently; that is, communicating differently in individual and group conversations (asking questions, listening, giving feedback).

Opportunities for collaboration do not automatically result in productive development work. Collaboration among teachers that is not purposeful or not skilfully done can be non-productive by focusing on war stories, complaints and telling tales of individual pupils. The leadership skills needed for collaborative work involve the ability to:

- develop a shared sense of purpose with colleagues
- facilitate group processes
- communicate well
- understand transition and change and its effects on each other
- mediate conflict
- develop positive relationships.

These perspectives and skills can be learned through the best forms of professional development; that is, observation and guided practice, coaching, skill-focused dialogue (talking through strategies and approaches) and training.

Enquiry-based use of information to inform shared decisions and practice

Such practices as reflection, dialogue, question-posing, enquiry (including uses of data), construction of new meaning and knowledge, and action are the renewal processes. Subject meetings used in this way can be highly stimulating. An agenda might call for the teachers to reflect on past successes and beliefs about teaching a particular topic. Questions are posed, 'Are the pupils experiencing this the way we think they are?' 'What are they learning?' 'How do we know?' An examination of pupil work can provide some interesting answers and these can be shared with other teachers at the next meeting. The dialogue focuses on making sense of pupil responses in reference to teachers' experiences and beliefs. Working together, the teachers might suggest alterations in how and where the topic is taught. This is where improvement in the quality of the craft of teaching takes place – through hearing and considering feedback from other teachers.

Action research and enquiry requires time but it also requires the rethinking of how we use the time that we have in schools. Teachers are very busy and time is precious; hence the creation of common time for dialogue and reflection needs to be planned. There is nothing more important than school improvement and thus time needs to be allocated to it.

Even in the best of schools, polarization (see Figure 2.1, quadrant 3) arises between those who are actively involved in change efforts and those who are holding back. A typical missing part in contemporary reform effort is communication and feedback systems. These 'feedback loops' are important to monitor development and inform others about progress. Information needs to be accumulated and reinterpreted as it moves through the school. It is essential that informed conversations take place about things that are happening in the school, how people are thinking and feeling about them, what ideas are occurring to them, and what meanings are emerging. It is in such a setting that leadership skills can be finely honed. Performed on a regular basis, the reciprocal learning processes can become familiar practice. Information will come to teachers in both formal (data and evidence) and informal (feedback loop conversations) ways. Consequently, opportunities to discuss and reflect are imperative if progress is to be made.

Roles and responsibilities that reflect broad involvement and collaboration

Growth in individual teacher capacity brings about a change in self-perception and roles. As roles change, new behaviours emerge: teachers can analyse data, be persuasive with parents or LEA personnel and ask critical questions. Teachers, particularly, no longer see themselves as responsible only for their classroom, but for the school as well. Old responses no longer work. As roles change, relationships change. People see each other in a new light. They recognize new skills and resources in people they have known for years. As the opportunities for new ways of being together emerge, relationships can cut across former boundaries that had been established. As more of 'who we are' becomes exposed, we find more in common with others.

Assuming responsibility for the agreements that the

school community has made represents an important role shift. Agreements usually require that everyone's role change and this can only be done with the full involvement of everyone affected. Otherwise, the head is cast as the 'implementer', the person who must force the change on the school through evaluation, supervision or monitoring. Decisions need to be accompanied by explicit agreements about responsibilities for each aspect of the innovation or development. If meaningful and purposeful collaboration is to occur then there has to be trust and transparency about roles and responsibilities.

Reflective practice/innovation as the norm
The cycle of enquiry described above has an essential reflective phase. Many forms of reflection must become an integral part of school improvement: reflection on beliefs, assumptions and past practice; reflection in action, in practice; collective reflection during dialogue and in coaching relationships. To create a norm of such habits of mind requires that time be available for reflection, that a 'language of reflection' (deliberate uses of phrases like: 'I've been thinking about, pondering . . .', 'When I reflect on . . .', 'I need to reflect about that') is part of the talk of the school. That reflection is demonstrated and honoured – but never used as an obstacle; rather it is the prelude before movement to action.

Reflection leads to the opportunity to 'run with' an idea, to see it through. If ideas are customarily blocked by the head, ideas are not likely to blossom on a regular basis. If a school community feels that an idea warrants a trial, many doors need to be opened to enable those teacher leaders (entrepreneurs) to transform the idea into reality. Innovators should be encouraged to involve other colleagues, to establish responsible criteria for success, and to create a realistic timeline for monitoring and evaluation.

High or steadily improving pupil achievement

The central focus of any school must be teaching and learning. Learning needs to be viewed as 'authentic'; that is, based on real tasks that have a relationship to work in society or in the family. Curriculum, instruction and assessment that are authentic have relevance, meaning and intrinsic worth. In this book, pupil achievement is broadly conceived and means:

- Academic achievement in authentically performed and assessed work whenever possible
- Positive involvement (good attendance, few suspensions, low dropout rate, high graduation rate, parent and pupil satisfaction)
- Sustained improvement over time. The longer that pupils were exposed to certain restructuring factors, the greater the improvement and the narrower the gap among pupils
- Resiliency behaviours (self-directing, problem-solving, socially competent, having a sense of purpose and future)
- Equitable gains across socio-economic groups; improvement regardless of gender, race or ethnicity
- Narrowed gaps between socio-economic groups.

Now consider how far the following dimensions of capacity building feature in your school?

1 Broad-based, skilful involvement in the work of leadership
2 Enquiry-based use of information to inform shared decisions and practice
3 Roles and responsibilities that reflect broad involvement and collaboration
4 Reflective practice/innovation as the norm
5 High or steadily improving pupil achievement.

In making this assessment, what should be the developmental priorities for your school and where should teachers' energy be placed?

Building leadership capacity for school improvement is essentially about constructing a better match between schools and young people. It is essentially about changing schools and the patterns of relationships that exist between staff and students. All too often, however, the students' voices are neglected in school improvement work and rarely are students given the opportunity to engage in or inform school improvement efforts. There is now an emerging evidential base that shows the contribution that student voices can make to school improvement. Students themselves have a huge potential contribution to make, not as passive objects but as active players in the education system. Consequently students need to be part of the drive for higher standards and achievement.

It is important that teachers listen to students and ensure that they have a voice in improvement efforts. In this respect, teachers must take the major responsibility for building leadership capacity in schools and ultimately for the work of school improvement. Teachers represent the largest and most stable group of adults in the school, and the most politically powerful. However, the role of the head is more important than ever. Sounds contradictory? The next chapter considers the role of the head in generating leadership capacity for school improvement.

3 BUILDING LEADERSHIP

CAPACITY: THE ROLE OF

THE HEAD

Increasingly, the best lead not by virtue of power alone, but by excelling in the art of relationship.

(Goleman 2002: 248)

Good leaders foster leadership at other levels.

(Fullan 2001: 10)

Introduction

If building leadership capacity requires distributing leadership to others why is the role of the head more important than ever? Even though teacher leadership is at the heart of building leadership capacity, the leadership of the headteacher is still the most vital and urgent form of intervention. This is because heads set the climate for improvement, they can empower others to lead and they can provide the much needed energy for change and development. Heads are the catalysts for change and development, they may not implement the changes but they enthuse others to take responsibility for change and development. They engage others in the emotional work of building collaborative, trusting relationships. Without this 'emotional climate' for change, even the most well conceived and received innovation is unlikely to succeed.

As Goleman (2002: 3) suggests 'great leadership works through emotions'. No matter what heads set out to do, whether it's creating strategy or mobilizing teachers to lead, their success depends on how they do it. It is much more difficult to build leadership capacity among teachers than to tell teachers what to do. It is categorically more uncomfortable to be full partners with teachers engaged in development work than to dictate or supervise from the apex of the organization. Even if they get everything else right, if the head fails to build positive relationships among staff and attend to the emotional life of the organization, nothing will work as well as it could or should (Harris 2002a). As Goleman (2002: 18) concludes 'in short, leaders' emotional states and actions do affect how the people they lead will feel and therefore perform'.

This is not to suggest that the head adopts a counselling stance with staff. That is to miss the point. The 'capacity building' head is someone who creates a climate of enthusiasm and flexibility, one where teachers feel invited to be at their most innovative, where they work together and give of their best. The capacity building head believes that every stakeholder in the school has the right, responsibility and capability to work as a leader. Such a perspective requires that the head is clear about their core values and confident in their own abilities in working with others. It will also require a high degree of emotional intelligence and empathy. Heads can no longer rely on sheer authority or control if they are serious about building learning communities in their schools.

The emotionally intelligent leader is self-motivating

and persists towards the goal of ensuring that all pupils achieve and learn. As heads, they are 'values-driven' and have a clear moral purpose that earns trust among teachers, pupils and parents (Day *et al.* 2000). Most importantly, they are 'resonant leaders' they are attuned to people's feelings and move them in a positive emotional direction (Goleman 2002). The capacity building head is a resonant leader but it is clear that heads confront the work of building leadership capacity from very different perspectives. Lambert (2002) offers us four different perspectives:

1 The Directive Head – who uses command and control
2 The Laissez-Faire Head – who makes decisions behind the scenes – not involving others
3 The Collaborative Head – who has opened participation yet is unsure how to involve those who don't choose to be involved
4 The Capacity Building Head – who creates meaning and shared knowledge through broad-based skilful involvement.

So let's just pause for a moment . . .

● What type of head are you/what type of head do you currently work for?
● What type of head would you like to be/what type of head would you like to work for?

While the evolution into effective leadership is developmental, these types cannot be said to be linear. In other words the directive head seldom becomes laissez-faire, although a collaborative head can become a capacity building head. The central issue is how they see their leadership role. If they view it as 'command and control' they will be unlikely to be the type of head who is interested in people or building capacity in their school. At best, the school will be stable as long as they remain there. At worse, their leadership approach will prove counterproductive as in the long term it will generate dependency and in some cases despondency.

Dependency relationships are most often observed in a quadrant 1 or the 'stuck school'. Unless this is directly challenged or changed it is unlikely that the school will improve. Realigning relationships from dependency to reciprocity is the major challenge of a school that is 'stuck'. Evidence about schools in difficulty that have improved point towards the central importance of changing the way people relate and work with each other (Harris and Chapman 2002). There are two types of dependency models that seem to develop in schools.

The first is a 'top-down' reliance on the head to make things happen and to take major decisions. The second is a type of co-dependency that operates where the head and the teachers depend on behaviours of the other to keep old patterns of behaviour in place. For example, the head signals that what is expected is compliance and for compliant behaviour the teachers are rewarded by being left alone to undertake their teaching. A bargain has been struck but one that is wholly counterproductive to school development, change and improvement. Consequently, it is important that the head monitors behaviours and relationships pretty carefully. But how do you break dependent or co-dependent relationships? As one head reflected:

> Teachers brought many problems to me. I worked hard to help them solve these problems but the better I became at this the weaker the school became. I soon realized that I had to encourage teachers to solve their own problems, find their own solutions and to make mistakes. By sharing our experiences we made better decisions and learned from one another.

In the past few decades much research has established the superiority of group decision making over that of even the brightest individual in the group. There is one exception to this position, when the group is co-dependent or lacks the ability to co-operate. Breaking through this 'co-dependency' arrangement requires heads and teachers to develop a different sort of relationship with each other. A few examples of successful strategies for breaking co-dependent relationships are as follows:

1 When a teacher asks permission of the head for something he or she wants to do, he or she can redirect the question by asking, 'What do you recommend?'
2 When a group of teachers remains silent, waiting for 'the answer' from a head, the head can say, 'I've thought about this issue in three ways . . . Help me analyse and critique these ideas' or 'I don't know the answers . . . let's think it through together'.
3 When the teachers have expectations about the role of the head and refuse to take on responsibilities 'because that is the head's job', the head can ask the teachers to explicitly negotiate in a subject meeting everyone's roles and responsibilities.

The first column of the Teacher Leadership Rubric in Appendix B describes multiple ways to recognize co-dependent and dependent behaviours.

The power and authority of the head can be used to reinforce and maintain dependent relationships. Alternatively, it can be used to establish and maintain processes that improve the leadership capacity of the school. In order to do the latter, a head can use formal authority to:

1 Develop a *shared vision* based on community values by involving teachers and community in reflection on their own cherished values, listening to those held by others, and making sense through dialogue of how to bring personal and community values together into a shared vision statement.
2 Organize for, focus and *maintain momentum* in learning dialogue basis.
3 Protect and interpret school *values*.
4 Work with all teachers to arrive at and *implement* school decisions.

These uses of authority will actually *redistribute* authority and power in a school so that a culture of teacher leadership within the school community can grow. The following strategies may be used by the head and teachers to cultivate such a culture and to build leadership capacity within the school:

- posing questions that hold up assumptions and beliefs for re-examination
- remaining silent, letting other voices surface
- promoting dialogue and conversations
- raising a range of possibilities, but avoiding simplistic answers
- keeping the value agenda on the table – reminding the group what they have agreed is important; focusing attention
- holding space and time for people to struggle with tough issues
- confronting data, subjecting one's own ideas to the challenge of evidence
- turning a concern into a question.

When a head, rather than a school community, solves all problems dependency behaviour creeps in and eventually becomes the norm at the school. In schools where decision making is shared, devolved and owned by many rather than the few the possibility for improvement and development is significantly enhanced. But how do heads devolve and distribute leadership? How do they equip teachers to be leaders in schools?

As the demand for schools to improve pupil achievement increases, the need for heads to cultivate broad-based, skilful participation in the work of leadership is essential. Heads who build and sustain leadership capacity share the following core beliefs:

1 Teachers, parents and pupils can be successful leaders when given the opportunity to lead.
2 School community members must experience success in leadership roles.
3 Leadership capacity will be enhanced when the head supports the leadership experience of others.

4 Building individual capacity of the many builds organizational leadership.
5 The ability to do this important work lies within the school membership.

These core beliefs revolve around the central notion of *distributed leadership* and *teachers as leaders*. Teacher leadership is primarily concerned with developing high-quality learning and teaching in schools. It has at its core a focus on improving learning and is a mode of leadership premised on the principles of professional collaboration, development and growth. Teacher leadership is not a formal role, responsibility or set of tasks, it is more a form of agency where teachers are empowered to lead development work that impacts directly on the quality of teaching and learning. Teacher leaders lead within and beyond the classroom, they identify with and contribute to a community of teachers and influence others towards improved educational practice.

The idea of extending leadership skills is powerful because it gives teachers recognition for the diverse but important leadership tasks they undertake on a daily basis. It also reinforces how these leadership activities influence the quality of professional relationships and standards of teaching within the school. Empowering teachers through teacher leadership improves their self-efficacy in relation to pupil learning. When teachers take on leadership roles it positively influences their ability to innovate in the classroom and has a positive effect on student learning outcomes. For example, at Highfields School (see chapter 6) teachers were engaged in curriculum development and timetabling decisions. They were leading on pedagogical development and innovative practices that directly influenced the quality of teaching and learning. Essentially, they were leading learning and leading learners.

In contrast to traditional notions of leadership, teacher leadership is characterized by a form of collective leadership in which teachers develop expertise by working collaboratively. For example, they may be teachers working together on a particular aspect of the Literacy Strategy or teachers who are jointly preparing new materials and resources for a new topic area. There are two key dimensions of teacher leadership; first, a focus on improved learning outcomes through the development work and, second, an emphasis on collaborative professional activity.

Teacher leadership incorporates three main areas of activity:

1 the leadership of other teachers through coaching, mentoring, leading working groups
2 the leadership of operational tasks that are central to improved learning and teaching
3 the leadership of pedagogy through the development and modelling of effective forms of teaching.

Teacher leaders can be curriculum developers, bid writers, leaders of a school improvement team, mentors of new or less experienced staff and action researchers with a strong link to the classroom. The important point is that teacher leaders are, in the first place, expert teachers, who spend the majority of their time in the classroom but take on leadership roles at times when development and innovation is needed. Their role is primarily one of assisting colleagues to explore and try out new ideas, then offering critical but constructive feedback to ensure improvements in teaching and learning are achieved. Collaboration is at the heart of teacher leadership, as it is premised on change that is undertaken collectively. For teacher leadership to be most effective it has to encompass mutual trust, support and enquiry. Where teachers share good practice and learn together the possibility of securing better quality teaching is increased.

One of the main barriers to teacher leadership concerns the 'top-down' leadership model that still dominates in many schools. The possibility of teacher leadership in any school will be dependent on whether the head and the senior management team within the school relinquishes power to teachers and the extent to which teachers accept the influence of colleagues who have been designated as leaders in a particular area. In order for teacher leadership to become embedded, heads will therefore need to become 'leaders of leaders' striving to develop a relationship of trust with staff, and encouraging leadership and autonomy throughout the school.

The requirements of generating and sustaining teacher leadership are:

- *Empowerment* and encouragement of teachers to become leaders and to provide opportunities for teachers to develop their leadership skills;
- *Time* to be set aside for teachers' leadership work, including time for professional development and collaborative work, planning together, building teacher networks, and visiting classrooms;
- *Opportunities* for continuous professional development that focuses not just on the development of teachers' skills and knowledge but on aspects specific to their leadership role, such as leading groups and workshops, collaborative work, mentoring, teaching adults and action research.

Headteachers have a key role to play in developing teacher leadership. Heads need to encourage teachers to become leaders, help teachers develop leadership skills and provide positive and limited constructive feedback. Headteachers need to create the infrastructure to support teacher leadership. They need to create opportunities for teachers to lead, to build professional learning communities and to celebrate innovation and teacher expertise. Hostility to teacher leaders can arise through factors such as inertia, over-cautiousness and insecurity. Overcoming these difficulties will require a combination of strong interpersonal skills on the part of the teacher leader and changes to the school culture that encourage change and leadership from teachers.

This hard work requires that heads and teachers alike serve as reflective, enquiring practitioners who can sustain real dialogue and can seek outside feedback to assist with self-analysis. These learning processes require finely honed skills in communication, group process facilitation, enquiry, conflict mediation and dialogue. Further, these skills are generally not the focus of professional preparation programmes and must be refined on the job. While a great deal has been written about collaboration, it would seem that achieving meaningful collaboration in schools is far from straightforward or easy. However, where teachers do collaborate and work together, there is evidence to suggest that classroom and school improvement is much more achievable. This necessarily involves building the capacity within the school for learning and improvement to take place. The most important aspect of building improvement capacity is working successfully with people.

Much of the vital work concerning school improvement identifies professional leadership as a critical factor in a school's ability to develop and change. This work highlights that heads in improving schools demonstrate some consistent habits of leadership which are compelling in their clarity. First, they gave central attention to building a school-wide collective focus on pupil learning of high intellectual quality. Second, they kept issues of teaching and learning at the centre of the dialogue and in doing so they built organizational capacity in their schools. Third, they consistently expressed the norms and values that defined the school's vision, initiated conversations and provoked teachers to think about that vision. Fourth, they created time for reflective enquiry and placed shared power at the centre of the school's development work. Finally, and of critical importance, they were conflict managers and politicians in the best sense, often seeking waivers, resources and policies to support the restructuring work. Essentially, they were teaching others in the school to understand what they were doing and to be able to behave in similar ways. These heads were the 'teachers of teachers' when it came to building leadership capacity.

While teacher leadership is the most distinguishing characteristic of a high leadership capacity school, the head is still the key individual in this process. The major undertaking of the head is to work with and through the adult community.

You might wish to consider the following questions:

- What does/what would teacher leadership look like in your school?
- What would be the main barriers? How could these be overcome?
- Who would you involve immediately in discussions about teacher leadership?
- What would you need to do/do differently to build leadership capacity in your school?

Building capacity for school improvement implies a profound change in schools as organizations. Of central importance in building learning capacity within organizations is the human perspective rather than system perspective. By placing people at the centre of change and development there is greater opportunity for organizational growth. Building capacity means extending the potential and capabilities of individuals and means investing in professional development. The metaphor of the learning community encapsulates the importance of fostering and harnessing the learning of all individuals: parents, students, governors and teachers. This can only be achieved with purposeful and deliberate intervention and action. Only in the most exceptional cases do learning communities evolve without planning, support and careful nurturing.

When a head uses the authority of his or her position to convene and sustain dialogue the school is on a sure road toward building leadership capacity. The head who enables teachers to build their own informal authority and demonstrate leadership behaviours will generate leadership capacity. The sum of these concerted efforts is *broad-based, skilful involvement* in the work of leadership.

But how does this happen? What does building leadership capacity look like in action? The next three chapters offer an insight into the processes and practices of building leadership capacity by presenting three case studies that illuminate how capacity building can be achieved in very different school contexts.

PART 2

BUILDING LEADERSHIP

CAPACITY: CASE STUDIES

4 HOW TO BUILD LEADERSHIP CAPACITY: MANOR PRIMARY SCHOOL

> Capacity building creates intellectual capital by emphasizing the development of knowledge, competence, and skills of parents, teachers and other locals in the school community.
>
> (Sergiovanni 2001: 48)

This chapter and the two subsequent chapters offer case studies of building leadership capacity in action. The three cases of Manor, Rookwood and Highfields can be related to the leadership capacity matrix in Figure 2.1 (p. 26) by aligning Manor with quadrant 1, Rookwood with a blend of quadrants 2 and 3, and Highfields with quadrant 4. No example will be entirely representative of your school, but the interaction of factors and symptoms may be strikingly familiar in at least one case. The purpose of these case studies is to provide insights into the way in which leadership capacity is generated in different types of schools. Manor is a primary school with *low* leadership capacity; Rookwood (the school from chapter 1) is a secondary school with *moderate* leadership capacity; and Highfields is a secondary school with *high* leadership capacity.

Each case study:

- outlines the critical features of building leadership capacity: the breadth of skilful involvement in the work of leadership; uses of information to inform decisions and practice; roles and responsibilities; reflective practice and innovation; and pupil achievement
- addresses those critical features of leadership capacity described above
- is followed by an analysis of how each school measured up to the critical features of leadership capacity and a discussion of actions essential to the improvement of that school. Questions that challenge each school can be found in Appendix A.

Manor Primary School is located on the edge of a large city, in a deprived community where unemployment is above the national average. At one time, the community was fairly homogeneous but the pattern has changed since the early 1980s. Now the families come from diverse backgrounds – diverse in race and culture, as well as income and land of origin. The school was built in the early 1950s to a design that requires pupils and adults to go outside in order to move from one section of the school to another. A central courtyard with wooden tables is used for lunch on sunny days; otherwise tables are set up in a small gym that includes a stage on one side. The windows are high and the old wine-coloured velvet stage curtain has seen better days. In the playground there are climbing frames and the school is surrounded by a large fence, which is broken in certain sections. There is a large amount of litter at the perimeter of the fence and the school borders on to a large council estate.

Many of the teachers have been at the school for many years. A few began their careers in this school and plan to retire from here. Rarely do the teachers talk about teaching and, when they do, it is about a specific problem pupil or an unsupportive parent. If asked, they would tell you that they are not unhappy as teachers at Manor Primary School. Similarly, they would say that the pupils are safe and happy. The value-added data and cognitive assessment test (CATs) score highlight underperformance and underachievement at the school. The standard assessment tests (SATs) results are below the local and national averages. The local education authority (LEA) is aware of the problem and pressure has been placed on the Head to introduce changes to improve performance. However, these have met with resistance from teachers who are 'fed-up' with new ideas and never ending changes.

The teachers in the school are clear about roles, responsibility and workload. They are clear that they need to focus attention on the classroom, maintaining the order and discipline essential to teaching. They are also clear that the leadership and management issues belong to the head and deputy – not to them. They accept certain requirements: attendance at once-a-month teachers' meetings, SATs meetings, parents' meetings and teachers' development days. Occasionally, the head will ask for monitoring and evaluation plans but mainly teachers are left alone to get on with their teaching.

For 15 years George Simpson had been the head at Manor. He was loved by almost everyone. His style might be characterized as that of a 'benevolent dictator'. He cared about people, told stories with the best of them and never embarrassed anyone by suggesting that they were not doing a good job. When George Simpson retired, the LEA wanted some new ideas at Manor. SAT scores had been slowly falling and so were the numbers on the roll. The school had barely missed being placed in special measures and parents were looking to the nearby primary as an alternative. The arrival of a new head, Sue Johnson was heralded as a new beginning for the school. While this was her first headship, Sue was able to describe some new and exciting ideas for Manor. She was enthusiastic and came with glowing recommendations. She seemed to be the right person for the job.

Since joining the school Sue has been fighting a rearguard action from teachers who are unhappy with the changes and innovations she has suggested. One teacher has threatened to resign while another has been signed off for three months with a stress-related illness. Things are far from good. In particular, the teachers resisted the practice that is essential to school improvement: they had not made time for collaborative planning and peer coaching. Peer coaching seemed the furthest from their minds and traditions! What had gone wrong? Certainly she had approached these developments carefully.

In her first teachers' meeting at this school she introduced her interests and intentions to move towards new ways of working together – collaboration, sharing, joint teaching. By the Christmas holidays she had laid out the plans, outcomes, and even the hoped-for effects on pupil achievement. The LEA felt that Sue was doing a 'great job'. During that first year, she had sent teachers to visit other schools and to attend workshops. She had even hired a couple of new teachers who had some knowledge of the innovations she was seeking to bring about. No one had come to her with serious objections. She had assumed assent when there were few questions in the teachers' meetings.

She realized, however, that the change agenda was pretty top down, an approach that she rationalized in two ways. Wasn't it more honest to be direct with a vision and an agenda than to act as though it was okay to continue as things were? And, her early attempts to implement some shared decision making had run into the only vocal opposition she'd experienced so far. A delegation of some of the long serving teachers had come to her and said that the head was expected to make decisions at Manor. Further, the teachers would oppose any practice that would expect teachers to 'do a manager's work'. Had she been wrong to interpret this session as granting her carte blanche? Frankly, Sue was relieved. She didn't have the time to implement all the innovations that she knew about and she certainly didn't want to dilute the reforms. Shared decision making could come later. One thing was crystal clear to Sue, heads were ultimately accountable for the success or failure in schools. Her fate as school leader rested on the success of these innovations. 'What should I do now?' she asked herself.

Manor had settled into quadrant 1 of the leadership matrix (Figure 2.1), signifying *low involvement* and *low skilfulness* in the work of leadership. The head had assumed an autocratic, albeit benevolent role. Relationships were primarily paternal in nature with rigidly defined roles, one-way communication, and codependent, compliant behaviours on the part of the teachers. Traditional practices stood fast against innovation and change. Memories of the good old days stood in as reflection. Pupil academic achievement was poor and irregular attendance and playground conflict were persistent problems. Poor pupil performance was blamed on unsupportive families, the challenging context and changing demographics.

Extensive work needs to be done at Manor School to move it forward to quadrant 4 of the leadership capacity matrix.

Analysis of the critical features of leadership capacity

Broad-based, skilful involvement in the work of leadership

Manor teachers have historically not been involved in the work of leadership. They have not taken responsibility for the growth and development of their colleagues, themselves, or even their pupils. They have used their influence to maintain the status quo, even to the point of enculturating new teachers into those norms. Since this influence requires certain skills, approaches for transforming reactive influence into positive influence are discussed below. Heads in this setting have been hired to meet the limited expectations held by the teachers. And the heads have found comfort in autocratic behaviours. Heads who did not fit the mould were soon advised about proper administrative roles.

Enquiry-based use of information to inform decisions and practice

Teachers have a firm sense of what they believe is happening to their pupils and their school. These perceptions are the direct outgrowth of ancient personal schema uncluttered by enquiry or evidence. They point to the changing demographics, pupil and family profiles dictating the inevitability of poorer performance. Teachers are not systematically involved in high-priority decisions about teaching and learning but do use information to plan events (How many parents came to parent's evening last year?), and SAT scores as the basis for selecting instructional materials.

Roles and responsibilities that reflect broad involvement and collaboration

Roles and responsibilities have remained traditional at Manor. Teachers focus on the classroom, social interactions with other teachers and maintenance of a reactive posture towards school and LEA requirements. Collaboration to improve teaching and learning is rare. When resistance on the part of the teachers proves insufficient, sabotage and undermining occur. The Head keeps the school running, manages the budget and wards off negative reactions from parents and the LEA. This 'protective' role is at the heart of the school's paternalism. Parents are not to get involved unless their activities raise money for the school. Pupils are 'receivers' of knowledge in the classic sense; direct teaching is the norm.

Reflective practice/innovation as the norm

Manor teachers see themselves as reflective, a word they liken to nostalgic 'remembering'. While remembering the history of the school is an important element in moving forward, these memories at Manor serve only to reinforce the status quo and pining for the good old days. Reflection done in the company of others for the purpose of rethinking practice cannot be found at Manor. Nor can innovation, unless imposed from above. Even imposed innovation, not supported and reinforced by collaborative work, soon becomes indistinguishable from regular practice.

High pupil achievement

Over the years, Manor has experienced small 'bumps' in pupil achievement scores, short-term improvements based on some technical changes. However, it is safe to say that pupil learning has not improved. In fact, as the changing demographics have brought children from different cultures and learning styles to the school, the old ways have become progressively less successful. Teachers do not take responsibility for pupil learning but blame failures on external forces. Therefore, the rhetoric of blame has become louder, signalling an inevitable community crisis in the making. This impending crisis has caused the LEA, and now the new head, to seek to try to bring about significant changes in classroom organization and teaching.

Discussion

Manor is the portrait of an entrenched or 'stuck' school. It is a vivid example of the systemic relationship among all elements in a school that interact to create an intractable situation. A paternalistic system; heads and teachers who thrived on the system the way it was; an unquestioning community – all of these factors have colluded to create a poor school with low leadership capacity. The educators, pupils and parents in this school are no different from those we find in many places. They find themselves captured by an environment that brings out certain behaviours that do not work in schools; for that matter, these behaviours do not work in any settings.

How do we get a handle on this situation? What are the critical points of intervention that will loosen the intractable parts and start the system breathing again?

The major challenge at Manor is to engage and focus the attention on pupil learning and building the responsibility connection. This is certainly not the only challenge confronting the school, but it is the most fundamental and difficult. Altering the beliefs and the culture at Manor requires a skilful change agent, either within or outside the school. Either person must have access to formal authority that can be used in the ways that have been described in the previous chapter. After three years, Sue was transferred to another school, so our discussion begins with a new head – a person more suitable for this context. While Sue had many strengths, she perceived her first level of work at Manor as innovation in teaching and learning; in fact, this first level of work needed to be attention to the dysfunctional teaching culture accompanied by some quick classroom successes.

The suggestions below are just that: not right answers, nor the only way. However, the new head who replaced Sue undertook the following strategies and tactics:

- In order to get to know the teachers she asked each person to come in before school started to get acquainted (all but one accepted). During this personal 'interview' she asked teachers about family and aspirations, how they felt about the school, what was of highest value to them, what they would like to see improved. She

listened   respectfully   without   expectations   or
declarations.

- She made some quick, short-term changes before school
started (replacing the antiquated photocopier, painting
the staffroom, buying round tables for the library). She
credited these changes to the teachers and rightly so, for
they had suggested them. As school began, she would
focus on short-term, visible changes that made people
feel listened to.

- Staff meetings included some of the leadership learning
processes described in Chapter 1. She particularly
sought to hold discussions that would bring to the surface the experiences, histories, perceptions and beliefs
of teachers.

- At the next meeting, she began by summarizing the
concerns she had heard from teachers during the personal interviews. She noted the quick changes that had
been made. 'Now, what is our next level of concern . . .
what are we still troubled by?' She asked teachers to
talk with each other and decide on a couple of key ideas.
The top issues were discipline and homework. She was
not surprised, for she knew that these two topics inevitably rose to the top when school improvement is initiated. 'If these are our main concerns, I feel very strongly
that we need to find out what the current situation is.
We have important evidence in your observations and
experiences. We also need to look at the achievement
data – and we need to know why children are not doing
their homework.'

- During the autumn term, the head gave top attention
to communication and visibility. She was in the corridors, staffroom, classrooms giving positive feedback.
Occasionally, when she felt a teacher was receptive, she
would offer a quick idea that she had used or seen used –
an idea that could be quickly and confidently implemented, such as three ways to get class started. She gave
attention to some powerful questions that she had used
to shift responsibility to teachers and empower them to
lead. Such questions included:

- How are the children doing? What are they learning today?
- This is interesting, tell me what you are doing here.
- What went on in your head when the pupils responded in that way?
- What do you look for in pupils' reactions that will tell you if pupils understood your instructions?
- How will you decide what to do next?
- What do you think might have caused that?
- As you envision the next lesson, what do you see yourself doing?

- The head gave particular attention to supporting and coaching new teachers who were hungry for feedback and ideas to improve their practice. Her coaching skills, plus a few 'mini-lessons' designed to address trouble spots, were welcome interchanges. She was careful not to intervene in the relationships that new teachers had with other more experienced teachers. However, new teachers became more bold in asking questions about teaching and learning of more experienced teachers.
- At staff meetings, she modelled how to manage productive meetings, giving her rationale for meeting designs. For example, 'Let's take a careful look at the agenda. We'll use ten minutes to brainstorm our ideas, then take turns advocating for our preferences. Can we agree to have the revised agenda completed by 9:30?'
- It seemed too early to this head to organize a sophisticated 'school improvement team', so she asked the teachers to nominate other teachers that they trusted to represent them on an 'school improvement advisory group'. This group began to operate in the second term of her first year. Its function was to serve as a clearing house for data and evidence about the school, to develop a process map (the sequence of events) for the work at hand, to plan staff meetings, to develop a communication system, and to converse about effective change processes.
- By January, relationships were forming in new ways and

some decisions had been made about discipline and homework (by the beginning of the third year, these decisions had been modified to make them more consistent with the vision of the school). In a half-day workshop, teachers convened to consider the school's vision and goals. The teachers summarized what they had learned about their history, values and interests. They examined evidence of pupil achievement, behaviour problems and teacher perceptions of problem areas. They developed a scenario about what they would like their school to be like for children (brainstorming key elements and combining them into a short description) and identified five goals to work with for the balance of the year. They agreed to review these decisions at the opening of school next year.

- The head knew that one of her most challenging undertakings would be breaking the codependent relationship between the head and the teachers. When the teachers asked for permission or came to her for the right answer, she redirected the conversation with questions that sought the teachers' insights, opinions and advice. When teachers proclaimed, 'this is not my responsibility', she refused to take it on herself but insisted on working it through with the teachers. She was careful not to signal limited expectations for the teachers and did not accept the circumscribed role that had historically been the head's responsibility. While engaged in this process of breaking codependencies, a danger is that more experienced staff could interpret these actions as 'weakness' or 'inability to make a decision'. To counteract such charges, it is important to model resolute, firm and decisive behaviours in appropriate areas in which heads exercise authority, such as convening the teachers to discuss pupil data or work or designing professional development opportunities.

The head casually announced that she expected to be at Manor for the 'long haul' – to see things through. Some observers might say that the head didn't accomplish much that first year. Manor did not witness major changes in pupil achievement, although there were fewer exclusions and fewer altercations on the playground. However, anger and hurt were diminished and diffused by respectful listening and involvement. Communication was open for the first time, including in the areas of school budget and government targets and expectations. The leadership structure was changing as teachers became involved with committees, the council and conversations. Attention was consistently being directed towards the teaching and learning agenda. The culture was beginning to change significantly.

The processes that made a difference in Manor Primary School can also be applied to other schools, including secondary schools. In Chapters 5 and 6, the cases of Rookwood Comprehensive School and Highfields School are analysed and discussed.

5 HOW TO BUILD

LEADERSHIP CAPACITY:

ROOKWOOD

COMPREHENSIVE SCHOOL

> Charismatic leaders inadvertently often do more
> harm than good because at best, they provide episodic
> improvement followed by frustrated or despondent
> dependency.
>
> (Fullan 2001: 1)

This book began with a dilemma posed by Rookwood
Comprehensive School – 'You see our Head left'. In this
chapter, that case is provided in more detail. The journey,
as well as the dilemma, is a common one. Rookwood is a
school caught mid-way in its improvement cycle. The
transitional issues that face Rookwood when the head
leaves are critical to our understanding of school change.
Equally critical is the role that was played by the LEA in

appointing a new head and re-framing its expectations for the school.

When Jennifer Fielding had a chance to sit down with her new colleague, Gary, the story of Rookwood began to unfold (see Chapter 1).

The story of Rookwood Comprehensive

In 1997, the LEA amalgamated two schools to form Rookwood Comprehensive School. This decision was primarily motivated by falling rolls over successive years at each of the two schools. Little thought or planning went into the question: 'What does it mean to be an amalgamated school?' The Chief Education Officer had eloquently described the new school possibilities at the decisive LEA meeting: 'a vibrant new schools with new vision and new opportunities for young people'. However, the school remained two schools in design and spirit. The split site meant that subject co-ordination and meetings were particularly difficult hence, the teachers split between the lower school and the upper school. They remained physically, emotionally and psychologically in two camps. Discipline was a frequent topic at heated teachers' meetings. Like so many split-site schools, trouble occurred as some pupils travelled between sites for different subjects.

Community expectations, particularly in the areas of discipline and career choices, varied between the two school sites. At one end of Rookwood's catchment area was the golf club and newly built homes that fronted on the green; at the other end was a council estate with low-cost housing. The community surrounding the two school sites was racially and culturally diverse with a recent upswing in families of modest means. The majority of parents in this suburban community commuted to a large city centre 30 miles away. In the spring of 1998, a new CEO was determined to see Rookwood become a 'single school'. After an exhaustive search, the LEA hired Martin

Saunders, an experienced school head. Clearly charged with the responsibility to 'make Rookwood into a successful and single school', Martin began his work at Rookwood.

Martin brought a track record for successful restructuring. He had a high respect for teachers and faith in the aspirations of parents and children. As teachers worked in their classrooms just before school opened and in the first few days of school, Martin visited each teacher. He asked those who had played a strong leadership role in each of the previous schools to drop by before school started. 'Fill me in,' he said. 'Tell me about what has happened here.' During the autumn, the teachers agreed to establish a new school improvement team. The team, made up of four key teachers and the head, agreed to meet on Tuesdays after school. In November, they attended team training at the LEA where such skills as communication, facilitation and conflict management were emphasized.

The team planned for a teachers' away-day in January to be held during two back-to-back teachers' development days. While there was some dissension over an overnight trip, strong LEA support encouraged almost full involvement. The January away-day was an historic event for Rookwood teachers. They talked about what they believed and valued, outlined a rough vision statement, and identified three small task forces to begin work on three top priority items:

1 behavioural issues
2 teaching and learning
3 parent involvement.

An initial plan for improved parent involvement was tentatively agreed, and the other reports were tabled for the autumn term. 'Perhaps we're moving too fast,' reflected Martin.

During the 2000–01 school year steady progress was made as the school improvement team kept the agenda focused. Six teachers volunteered to explore peer coaching. A pupil leadership team was formed that met before school. Martin took on a 'servant' role in relationship to the improvement team and task forces. He gathered data and provided it to the teams. He also served as a clearing house for information and communication. A weekly letter updated teachers on the progress being made by teacher leaders. The deputy head continued to concentrate largely on discipline, pupil activities and his share of teacher evaluations. Pockets of innovation (pairs of peer coaches and observations in other classrooms; three classrooms using project-based learning) were growing and he could observe improvements in many classrooms, particularly with inductive and co-operative learning strategies.

While little change could be expected so early on, attendance, behaviour and performance levels were all improving. At teachers' meetings, teachers led discussions on the progress they were making in each area of improvement. Martin knew that some teachers were holding out – occasionally grumbling about expectations to 'lower standards in order to become friends to these kids', even though he and several teachers said more than once that higher standards were the goal. He continued to treat those individuals with respect and trusted that they would come to share his sense of urgency about school reform.

The LEA was pleased with the progress at Rookwood. They could see the improvements and parents were becoming more positive in the comments they made. No doubt that the community was beginning to have faith in the work being done at the school. Rookwood teachers were invited to participate in LEA workshops and presentations. It was in such a vibrant and lively period that Jennifer Fielding had decided to transfer to Rookwood.

In the spring of 2001, Martin announced that he was resigning to accept another headship. He was somewhat surprised at the teachers' response. Those teacher leaders with whom he had worked most directly were happy for him but felt a sense of betrayal. 'You're strong enough to continue this work,' he argued. 'We are over the major hurdles. You are skilled in leading the school. And the LEA has assured me that they will find a head who will be a compatible partner and continue the agenda you've set for yourselves.'

A new head was not appointed until August, so plans for the beginning of the school year were not well thought out. He had little opportunity to talk with teacher leaders or anyone on the teaching staff. Those who had participated in leading the restructuring efforts seemed disillusioned and angry in the autumn of 2001. Those who had resisted felt vindicated.

Rookwood can be understood as a blend of quadrants 2 and 3 of the leadership capacity matrix in Figure 2.1. It is a combination of a 'fragmented school' with some emerging features of a 'moving school'. Martin had been a thoughtful, focused educator but his behaviour revealed three shortcomings that arrested progress at the school:

1 He and a few teachers were the primary communicators. And he was the central source of data.
2 He was unable to confront and mediate the growing opposition among some teachers.
3 He left the school too early in the reform process.

Therefore, there were limited uses of data for decision making and a lack of coherence between improvement initiatives. Teachers were increasingly polarized as the chasm developed between teacher-leaders and teachers who perceived themselves on 'the outside'. Pockets of innovation had also resulted in pockets of improvement in pupil performance. Overall, by the third year, pupil achievement showed a slight improvement. As in the case of Manor, the work at Rookwood needed to move the school towards the critical features of quadrant 4 of the leadership capacity matrix.

Critical features of leadership capacity

Broad-based, skilful involvement in the work of leadership

By the time Martin left the school, about 30 per cent of Rookwood teachers were actively involved in some aspects of the reform. Another 20 per cent (primarily including new teachers) were sympathetic and co-operative. However, pockets of resistance were strong. The involved teachers had become skilled in planning sequences of events, designing and facilitating interactive meeting agendas and reflecting on and assessing their progress. However, certain terrain had been occupied only by the head, or not explored at all. Foremost among these untouched skill areas were conflict management (surfacing, confronting and working through conflict), communication and enquiry. Martin had assumed the major responsibility for communication and for collecting and organizing evidence about the school. When respect and courtesy had not been sufficient to win over reluctant teachers, he rode it out, hoping that things would change.

Enquiry-based use of information to inform shared decisions and practice

While the school improvement team used information and evidence to make decisions, they had not involved other members of the teachers in the enquiry process itself. Data and evidence had been discovered and synthesized by the head. Data were understood as numbers, while the richness of qualitative data (observations, interviews, focus groups) was not accorded the same importance. Teachers had yet to trust their own observations and interpretation of pupil work as important evidence. The general communication system was composed of written information, a one-way approach that did not seek feedback, interactions and new interpretations. Staff meetings did promote interaction and dialogue, critical features of a communication system, but this pattern did not continue between meetings. The peer coaching teams were able to generate insights and strategies that improved practice in the pilot classrooms. A system for sharing these improvements was not yet in place. When attempts were made to share the results of these collaborative efforts, resistant teachers became sarcastic or silent – either action served to intimidate the experimenting teachers.

Roles and responsibilities reflect broad involvement and collaboration

There were some important role changes among participating teachers. These teachers were beginning to see themselves as facilitators of adult learning, change agents, reform planners. They were sensitive barometers within the changing culture. As decision makers and problem solvers, they had developed meeting agendas that were crisp yet allowed for consideration of evidence and dialogue. Their actions and instincts were collaborative and open. As a group, teacher roles included the full spectrum of professional role development. At one end of the spectrum, teachers were focusing exclusively on the classroom as lone practitioners, assuming a rather passive role in group gatherings. Many teachers were in transitional phases, beginning to work collaboratively to reflect on practice and engaging in productive dialogue in organized meetings. At the professional end of the spectrum, teachers were taking responsibility for leading the reforms, implementing community decisions, mentoring new teachers and reaching beyond the school to influence the LEA and the region. The problem here was that this process needed at least one more year to include enough teachers to take root.

The role of the deputy head was narrowly defined. Since he focused primarily on pupil behaviour and activities, he did not understand the whole picture of the restructuring effort; therefore, it was difficult for him to provide transitional leadership when the head left. The head had retained the major leadership role, including responsibility for enquiry and communication, and especially including communication with the LEA.

Reflective practice/innovation is the norm

While there were strong pockets of reflective practice, such practice was not the norm. The peer coaching teams were making time to talk about their work and learning from each other. Overall, observation of practice was in its initial stages. Other than at teacher development days and meetings, there was no organized time for peer coaching, team development and other reflective practices. The school and the LEA had not found acceptable ways to support school day reflective time. More time and compromise were needed to work this out.

High pupil achievement

Rookwood pupils were beginning to make small gains. While little difference had occurred on GCSE performance, A–Cs were below the LEA average, behaviour factors such as attendance, classroom discipline and referrals, and school-ground conflicts were showing improvement. Pupils were more involved in goal setting and decision making, including creating plans for their own performance. In general, however, pupils and parents were still outside the information/feedback loop. That is, parents were informed but not involved in setting new performance goals.

The innovations had brought about more pupil-centred classrooms. Content remained important, but more of the learning was coming from pupil enquiry and experimentation. Authentic assessment was being talked about; a pilot portfolio was underway in English classes. Classroom improvements and pupil achievements were in evidence but were not sustained – a testimony to inconsistent teacher involvement in improvement efforts at Rookwood Comprehensive School.

Discussion

The governors hired John Trevor as their new head. John was an experienced school head, but he knew that this challenge was unique. After meeting with teacher leaders and many others, both within and outside the school, he assessed the challenges to be first, one of reclaiming and building on the reforms and commitments established in the first three years; and second, breaking through the barriers inhibiting further progress and change, and assuring teachers that he would be around to see it through. He would seek to define his role as colleague with teacher leaders at the school, supporter of current reforms, learner and facilitator. It would be important for him to work as a collaborative peer, not 'reclaiming' any of the authority that had already been redistributed.

The teacher leaders became John's coaches, while John was able to bring some new skills in change and conflict management, coaching and communication to the team. In order to confront the challenges before them, John and the teacher leaders undertook the following approaches and strategies:

- John used many of the trust building approaches used by the previous head. He personally reached out to teachers, getting to know and listen to them without judgement. Yet, the team knew that they could not wait until trust was established with John (such as at Manor) to make some major moves.
- The school improvement team asked the staff to conduct a process to select two new members. At an all-day Saturday planning session, the team reviewed their

achievements, selected their priorities and refocused their agenda.

- John – and the team – sought to bridge the distance between staff based at the two sites by 'pacing and leading'. This meant that in each of their interactions and in staff meetings they would recall and recapture where they had been in order to build a pathway to 'what happens next?' For instance, a team member might say, 'You've made great strides at broad-based involvement here with our improvement team, ad hoc groups, coaching and interdisciplinary teams. How will we get even more people involved?'
- As a critical aspect of the pace and lead approach, team members often restated the school's vision as they talked. Team members sat down with teachers to seek clarification of the meaning of the vision statement, particularly in reference to what they hoped for in pupil achievement. They would often ask, 'How will we know when we are doing this? What will it look like?'
- The improvement team and teachers were unfamiliar with alternative communication processes. They were of like mind, however, that this was an area that needed attention. One-way communication had reinforced passivity. John framed the development process by working with the leadership team to pose a few critical planning questions:

  1 How can we organize ourselves to hold personal conversations with each teacher about issues and decisions?
  2 What decision-making processes provide opportunities for the teachers and broader community to interpret and discuss issues, thereby accumulating feedback for the key groups involved?
  3 What forms of written communication are efficient in assisting group understanding and feedback?
  4 How can the teachers organize, both in meetings and outside of meetings, to maximize interactions about issues important to the school?

5 How can we involve the community and LEA in these communication processes?

6 How can we ensure that our communication system includes opportunities for reflection, dialogue and enquiry?

- The team assessed the nature of the struggle of teachers with each other. Teacher leaders noted that some resistant teachers had significant personal power. They knew just what to say – and when – to quiet – their colleagues. John began to model positive confrontation and to coach teacher leaders in mediation and conflict management work.
- In the limited ventures into the use of data to inform decisions and practice, teachers had tended to define data as numbers. While these data made important contributions to the work at Rookwood, this perception also limited the deeper understandings that can be discovered through qualitative research approaches. John suggested that they redefine data more broadly as 'evidence' and talked about the validity of pupil work products and performances, classroom observations, interviews, focus groups and dialogue sessions.
- The team was able to introduce structured reflective practices at staff meetings. Team members introduced an abridged form of the 'protocol', conversations about pupil work, case studies written by teachers about action research as an approach to whole school change, and actively supported the expansion of peer coaching. Recognizing that the teachers needed to assess what they were doing and discover some of their own innovations, they redefined the enquiry process as a legitimate path to their own self-renewal.
- The improvement team and the other teachers clearly defined and articulated what they meant by 'LEA support'. High on the list was the need for 'prime time' for adult collaborative work. (For other aspects of this strategy, see Chapter 6.)
- The teacher leaders agreed to break the 'norm of silence'

(that is 'I won't talk with you about anything you're uncomfortable with.'). They knew that comprehensive implementation of the school's reforms required that everyone get on board.

By the following summer, three teachers took up positions at other schools. Other teachers assumed responsibility for implementation of their agreed-on innovations (advisement, performance-based assessment, peer coaching, parent involvement). While these approaches and strategies took time and had to be undertaken in a sensible sequence, Rookwood did not lose much momentum in its reform efforts. Thanks to teacher leadership and an experienced and reflective head, Rookwood was able to consolidate its gains and move forward towards quadrant 4 of the matrix to become an improving school.

But what happens if you are already a school that is improving? How do you sustain improvement over time? The focus of the next case study is Highfields school – a school that is improving and is firmly located in the fourth quadrant of the matrix.

6 HOW TO BUILD
LEADERSHIP CAPACITY:
HIGHFIELDS SCHOOL

> It is now clear that for school improvement, leadership needs to focus on two dimensions – the teaching and learning focus on the one hand and capacity on the other.
>
> (NCSL 2001)

Situated on the northern boundary of the city, Highfields serves an area described as 'one of serious social need'. Eight years ago Highfields faced possible closure. Demographic trends coupled with a poor image in the community meant that the school had been steadily losing pupils and staff for several years. In January 1993 a new headteacher was appointed with the brief to address the decline.

A rapid period of research – interviews with staff, questionaires to pupils, parents, local community and meetings with local primary school staff – produced a picture of a school that was seen as caring but which lacked challenge. Three clear aims were quickly established:

1 To improve the school's image in the community.
2 To develop the links with the primary schools.
3 To tackle the culture of underachievement.

The threat of possible closure, replaced after the first 12 months with the 'threat' of an OFSTED inspection, proved to be powerful factors in focusing the minds of staff within the school. A new staffing structure, clear policies, new uniform, well-structured Code of Conduct, mentoring programmes all began to show positive effects. Pupil numbers began to increase, examination results improved and the 'what-can-you-expect of . . .' culture was being successfully challenged. Within the OFSTED report the quality of teaching and learning emerged as a major issue. It was recognized that for lasting improvement the school needed to bring about more sustainable change focused on the classroom.

At the critical moment the school learned of the Improving the Quality of Education for All (IQEA) project (*www.iqea.net.com*). IQEA places its main emphasis on building the internal capacity for change and development. It focuses primarily on improving student learning outcomes and achievement by creating the conditions at school and classroom level that promote change and development (Hopkins *et al.* 2002). In IQEA teacher development is given the highest priority and quality staff development and training is a major component across the programme. Staff development is school-based and classroom focused. The main thrust of the work is to equip teachers to manage classroom change, development and improvement. Teachers are actively encouraged to build their own professional communities both within and outside the school. Even though some generic programmes of training are provided for participating schools in each project, emphasis is still placed on teacher collaboration and networking. The net result of this activity is not only the sharing of good practice but the establishing of professional development communities within the school that can sustain and maintain development.

Phase one

The project's emphasis on teaching and learning at the heart of sustained improvement was felt to be in total accord with where Highfields was in its particular stage of development. This approach to school improvement called for, among other things, the establishment of a group, known as the cadre, to act as the initial change agents. The first cadre group consisted of the head and seven volunteers – a deputy head, two heads of department and four main professional grade teachers. All areas of the curriculum except one were represented. At this time, several members of the cadre attended a summer school on the subject of 'models of teaching' run by the University and soon realized that the inductive model offered a possible way to address the issues facing the school. This was partially because it was a new approach, and therefore offered exciting possibilities, and because it was applicable across the whole curriculum it seemed an ideal place to start.

For the cadre group, the first stage was to learn more about the model, to practise it and to observe each other. Lessons were then videoed and, when they felt ready, a day's INSET session was prepared for the whole staff. The model was explored inductively, videos shown and opportunities created for staff to begin to practise using the model with other groups of staff.

In order to encourage other people to adopt this approach, staff were clustered into small groups with a member of the cadre attached to each one to provide support and guidance. As well as working with their support groups, staff also worked within their departments, reviewing schemes of work to see where the inductive approach might be used to greatest effect and planning lessons accordingly.

By now the school was approaching the end of the first year, consequently, the whole process was reviewed and several clear 'messages' emerged:

- the importance of creating a regular *time* for the cadre group to meet
- the need for time for staff to *learn* new models, to prepare new materials, to observe each other and visit other schools to observe good practice
- The need for time to develop *teacher leadership*.

Creating more time required a radical rethinking of the way time was currently used in the school. The problem was resolved in the following ways:

- The meeting structure was reviewed and staff meetings, for example, were replaced by staff development time. Alternative methods were used to disseminate information. All remaining meetings, such as departmental meetings, were to devote 50 per cent of the time to development issues relating to teaching and learning.
- Staff were encouraged to 'bank' some non-contact time by covering other colleagues. This time was then pooled so that all staff, either as individuals or departments, were given half-day slots for development.
- Members of the senior management team were to provide a percentage of the cover time each fortnight, which could be booked by staff.
- Adults other than teachers were to be used to supervise exams and thus free departments.

The careful positioning of INSET, twilight and staff development meant that teachers were now meeting approximately every four weeks to look at development issues focused on teaching and learning. It was also agreed, following consultation with the staff, to broaden the range of activities.

Phase two

It was during the second year that the real benefits of this approach to school improvement became apparent. Working in pairs and triads, the cadre used the expertise of university and LEA personnel plus their own reading and research to develop their expertise in areas as diverse as the major components of a well-structured lesson, co-operative group work, whole class teaching, formative assessment, creating the learning classroom. The aim was to encourage staff to develop at their own pace, while providing the necessary expertise and support within a climate that encouraged risk taking.

Preparing to enter its third year of the IQEA project, the school was informed of the imminent OFSTED inspection. This led to a period of consolidation rather than innovation and change. The inspection results were better than hoped for. OFSTED deemed that, 'Teaching is a strength of the school'. A total of 97 per cent of lessons were judged satisfactory or better, 64 per cent were good or better and 28 per cent were very good or excellent. This was in sharp contrast with the picture four years earlier when only 75 per cent of lessons were judged satisfactory and less than 30 per cent were good or better.

As compared with three years ago, the school is in a position where:

- Teaching and learning is acknowledged to be at the heart of the school's development agenda.
- Classrooms are more open and people more willing to observe and be observed.
- Staff are developing a language to talk about teaching and learning.
- People feel part of the development process. They are involved in making it happen not just the unwilling recipients.

As OFSTED noted: 'The school is successfully challenging the non-achievement culture, noted in the

previous OFSTED Report, through its major focus on raising the quality of teaching. This is having a major impact
on pupils' attainment and progress.'

School improvement researchers have consistently
stressed the importance of teachers' commitment to
a form of teacher development that extends teaching
repertoires and engages teachers in changing their practice (Hopkins *et al.* 2002). IQEA is an example of a
project that reflects this form of teacher development
because it involves teachers in 'a rigorous mutual examination of teaching and learning' (Little 1993). There is
sufficient evaluative evidence from IQEA to show that
when teachers are engaged in dialogue with each other
about their practice then meaningful teacher learning
occurs.

Much more is now known about the conditions under
which teachers develop to the benefit of themselves and
their students. The problem remaining is how to integrate
teacher and school development, as considerable fragmentation still exists between these two areas. If the boundaries are to be transcended then strategies for powerful
change are required that restructure and integrate teacher
development and school improvement. From a theoretical
and empirical point of view, the classroom is the pre-
dominant place in the school where learning and teaching
take place, and in this way the classroom level is more
important for learning outcomes than other levels in
education (Creemers 1994).

Phase three

The current phase of Highfields's development is
intrinsically linked to a bid for and subsequent award of
Technology College Status. Highfields has interpreted
Technology College status as a tool for focusing on further
improvement. It also has provided the opportunity for
the school to maintain a classroom focus, further developing and refining classroom processes in relation to

community, capability and capacity. Strong links have been developed with local primary schools. ICT teachers regularly visit these schools and teach collaboratively with primary colleagues. The school has made attempts to engage the local community and raise the profile of the school. Links with parents have become increasingly positive and attendance at parents' evenings and events continue to rise.

Devolution of power and responsibility has contributed to improvements in the capability of staff especially at middle management level. Efforts have been made to improve the alignment of the organization at different levels and to build inter-departmental teams, creating multiple channels of communication and relationships based on higher-level networks, rather than relying on traditional linear hierarchies. These internal networks serve to develop staff, plan for succession, share ideas and develop consistent good practice across the school. The school has planned for and is implementing further structural changes that will result in a flatter management structure and further disperse the leadership within the organization.

Critical features of leadership capacity

Highfields School is an example of a school that is a professional, living community (see Figure 2.1, p. 25). It is a 'moving' school with high levels of leadership skill and a high degree of involvement. Initially, the head had used his influence to encourage the school to join IQEA and to break through the traditional blaming and avoidance stance. Schools that join IQEA sign up to a core set of principles and a way of working that embodies action research, dialogue and reflective enquiry. When we joined the story, the head was no longer the primary 'mover and shaker'. Instead, teachers, pupils and parents held significant leadership roles within the school. In addition to their new roles, their participation involved skilful dialogue, enquiry, reflection and problem solving. The cadre group was responsible for initiating innovation and change in the school. Their role was largely a facilitative role embracing others in decision making about change and ensuring change happened.

In the school the flow of information is open, fluid and complex involving multiple forms of personal, small group interactions and decisions. Roles and responsibilities at Highfields are also fluid. Teachers move in and out of leadership roles. The cadre is not a permanent group and there is a turnover of membership as new tasks and decisions arise. All staff, including support staff, are involved in decisions about the future direction of the school. In many ways, the school can be described as a 'learning community' where opportunities for professional development, joint decision making and meaningful collaboration are enhanced (See Chapter 9).

Critical features of high leadership capacity

Broad-based, skilful involvement in the work of leadership

The majority of the Highfields School teachers have become skilful leaders. Their resolve to improve their school led to greater involvement, peer observation and coaching, visits to other schools, networking and regional conferences, and training. Pupils and parents are involved; leadership skills are growing strong within both groups. Experiences with the work of leadership shifted attitudes and perspectives from passivity to active engagement, from blame to responsibility, and from cynicism to hopefulness.

Highfields School has a strong vision and this is emphasized in its programme for new teachers, as well as new pupils, parents and administrators. Such enculturation is a concerted effort to enable newcomers to understand how Highfields School works and the expectations held there for new community members.

Enquiry-based use of information to inform shared decisions and practice

Highfields School uses a school-wide collaborative action research model in their cycle of improvement. They believe that everyone, not just individuals or small elite groups, needs to be involved. The learning process involves reflection, enquiry, dialogue and action – much as we have seen in the story above. Decision making and practice are both informed by the information emerging from the enquiry process as well as by an open and fluid flow of information from within and outside the school.

Roles and responsibilities that reflect broad involvement and collaboration

Roles are blended and complementary as well. Roles are defined by the needs of the pupils and the broader school community. Teachers serve as mentors and coaches to each other and to pupils and parents. The head and senior management team model leadership behaviours, particularly by asking critical questions, convening dialogue sessions and focusing the agenda. Authority and resources are redistributed so that teachers, pupils and parents often act as entrepreneurs, taking responsibility for seeing an idea through to its conclusion. Roles at Highfields School are also fluid. One can move in and out of active leadership without condemnation. Teachers as a whole take responsibility for the implementation and evaluation of community decisions, involvement in professional development, and engagement in the additional work of leading a community of learners.

Reflective practice/innovation as the norm

Reflection, enquiry and dialogue are inherent within the school. The processes have become second nature within the school. Collegial professional development plans have replaced most aspects of traditional teacher evaluation. These professional development plans involve collaborative planning and interactive learning, including peer coaching. A natural product of reflection, enquiry, dialogue is that innovations are tied to the unique context of the school. Innovation arises from real concerns and issues generated from within the school community.

High pupil achievement

Pupils are achieving well at Highfields School. Evidence of self-direction is strong. Pupils are proactively forming learning plans, outlining and completing exhibitions, locating community sites in which to provide service, initiating relationships and requests for assistance, and assisting other pupils with their work. Pupils also occupy leadership roles through the school council and working group participation. Their participation in decision making is seen as being of paramount importance and an indicator of the way in which the school aims to build a learning community for all, including teachers, pupils and parents.

Discussion

While Highfields School still has room to grow, its most interesting challenge is the sustainability of the processes and programmes that warrant its recognition as a school with high leadership capacity. One major threat to sustainability has been superbly addressed: the capacity of Highfields School for self-renewal is not the sole possession of a few people or one head. Leadership is broadly based and skilful. The school will not crumple if a few key individuals leave.

Two major sustainability issues are:

1 Sustaining the energy and commitment of teachers who are actively involved in the school
2 Avoiding the danger of 'implosion' from too much change too quickly.

The teachers and community of Highfields have identified the following approaches and strategies designed to address these two issues and sustain their accomplishments at the school. They have undertaken several of these – they cannot all be undertaken at once – and will phase in others. As a school community, Highfields will:

● Attend to its own development by continually reflecting on their own processes and progress.
● Keep scheduled time and an organizational structure for reflection, enquiry and dialogue.
● Arrange for teachers to secure training in advanced coaching strategies to strengthen their listening and questioning skills with pupils and each other as well as to prepare them for the mediative challenges above.
● Develop professional products and publications such as dialogue guides, professional development plans, position papers, workshop agenda and journal articles in order to share and disseminate the work at Highfields.
● Blend established practices with process modifications in order to keep the work vibrant, not routine. For instance, sharpen dialogue, enquiry and reflection processes by adding new skills and strategies.
● Never lose the pupil focus. Since children, families and society are always changing, so must a school.

A few afterthoughts

Highfields School will overcome future challenges by nurturing its learning community through persistent professional dialogue that enables teachers to challenge assumptions and affirm their fundamental need to care about their pupils and their own worth. This process requires teachers who will stay with the process long enough to learn some new ways of doing business and a head with a capacity to use authority to convene and support the dialogue rather than to give the answers and commands. The next chapter reflects on the process and practice of building leadership capacity for school improvement.

PART 3

BUILDING THE CAPACITY

FOR SCHOOL

IMPROVEMENT

7 BUILDING LEADERSHIP

CAPACITY FOR

SUSTAINED SCHOOL

IMPROVEMENT

> The promise of sustainable success in education lies not in training and developing a tiny elite, but in creating entire cultures of distributed leadership throughout the school community
>
> (Hargreaves, A. 2001)

In Chapters 4, 5 and 6, the school case studies set forth the major issues and dilemmas inherent in building leadership capacity for sustained school improvement. The approaches and strategies were tailored to those specific situations, although most of them hold value for all schools. But how do you get started on building leadership capacity for school improvement? What are the basic conditions under which all schools can engage in this work?

This chapter gives a few guidelines. There is no five- or ten-step plan, but there is a set of conditions that need to be attended to if leadership capacity is to grow. Some of these conditions may already be in place in your school, others will need your explicit attention. Use these guidelines to help you decide where and how to proceed.

Keep in mind that these guidelines are systemic; that is, they are connected in such a way that they form a dynamic relationship to each other and to the set. If some essential conditions are missing, others will become dysfunctional. However, these conditions are not narrowly prescriptive. There are multiple strategies for enquiry and problem solving. You will want to choose those best suited for your school and your teachers.

Let us remind ourselves that school improvement rests on a number of key assumptions:

- schools have the capability to improve themselves
- school improvement involves cultural change
- there are school-level and classroom-level conditions for change
- school improvement is concerned with building greater capacity for change.

Successful school improvement, as we have seen from the case studies, involves building leadership capacity for change by creating high levels of involvement and leadership skilfulness. The crucial point is that in order to build leadership capacity there needs to be a focus and continued emphasis on the leadership capabilities of all those within the school community – parents, pupils and teachers.

Creating sustainable school improvement means, first understanding the *culture* that exists in the school and second deciding on *strategies* for change and development that match the particular context. Within the process of school improvement, no one can tell people what to do. They have to be allowed to search for their own solutions and to instigate and manage change inside their own institutions. However, while school improvement blueprints may be in short supply, the key levers for improvement are clearly evident in the research literature concerning successful school improvement. These 'school improvement levers' are as follows.

Build good relationships

You will have noticed in the case studies that a great deal of importance is given to building trusting environments with solid relationships. We need to know each other as whole individuals: as colleagues, friends, parents, citizens. It is through these relationships that we can understand and respect each other's experiences, values and aspirations. Within such authentic relationships, our self-concepts and world views nestle and evolve. Our fundamental beliefs can be made public and discussed when we know we can count on others to respect us for who we are, regardless of our differences. This is a tall order in any organization, but even more vital in schools since we expect educators to form such relationships with pupils as well.

Authentic relationships are fostered by personal conversations, frequent dialogue, shared work and shared responsibilities. As individuals interact with each other, they tend to listen across boundaries – boundaries erected by disciplines, grade levels, expertise, authority, position, race and gender. In the section, Organise the school for leadership work, below, one of the criteria for selecting governing and work structures is to maximize interactions that allow for relationship building.

Trust is built and experienced within the context of multi-faceted communication systems such as those described earlier in this book. A communication system needs to be open and fluid, include feedback loops and be practised by everyone in the school. The central function of such a system is to create and share information and to interpret and make sense of information as it is generated and shared. Rumour is a persistent communication barrier in most schools; assertive information sharing can disarm those who create and fuel rumours.

This is not to suggest that we wait to know each other well before getting on with the work of school improvement. Building relationships occurs before new work is commenced, but they primarily work themselves through as we move towards a shared purpose of schooling.

Assess teachers and school capacity for leadership

Building leadership capacity is primarily a function of the five critical features of schools described in previous chapters. To remind ourselves once again of these features, they are:

1 Broad-based, skilful involvement in the work of leadership
2 Enquiry-based use of information to inform shared decisions and practice
3 Roles and responsibilities that reflect broad involvement and collaboration
4 Reflective practice and innovation as the norm
5 High pupil achievement.

The dispositions, knowledge and skills essential to the achievement of these features are learned in a variety of ways: by observation and reflection, modelling and metacognition (the mentor/coach talks aloud about the process strategies in use), collaborative work and training. Learning that is embedded in the work itself is far more powerful than decontextualized In-Service Training (INSET).

A listing of the needed dispositions, knowledge and skills can be found in the teachers' assessment survey (see Appendix A, also Appendix B, A Rubric for Assessing Teacher Leadership). This survey is useful for an entire school, a school improvement team or other small groups. Before completing the survey, the teachers need to understand the source of the ideas and the concept of leadership capacity as a context for understanding and responding to the survey items.

It is helpful to have each individual plus one or two trusted colleagues complete this survey. Work in groups of three, asking each person to complete his or her own survey and two others. Talk through the results, looking for agreements and discrepancies. Discuss the discrepancies, asking for examples that influenced the responses. This 'triangulated' feedback can be a powerful learning experience for teachers and can lead to genuine commitments for skill building.

Once the survey is administered and self-scored, the results have implications for individual professional development plans and school-wide professional development. A wallchart that summarizes the teachers' three or four highest needs can show a pattern and direction for teachers' learning – including teachers' training. It can also serve as a decision-making tool for teachers to select among participant options. For instance, 'Am I prepared to serve on the Leadership Team, Research Group, an action research team? Organize a support group for new teachers? Serve as a process observer or a peer coach?'

Develop a culture of enquiry

A basic human learning need is to frame our work and our lives with big questions: How can I reach my pupils better? What really works? How will I define myself as a teacher? A commitment to a culture of enquiry responds to this need by allowing a forum in which we surface and describe our most compelling questions. This is often not the norm in schools where teaching and learning have become technical and routinized. When we pose questions of relevance, we re-energize ourselves and focus our work together.

In this pursuit, it is essential that the reciprocal processes of leadership – reflection, enquiry, dialogue and action – be integrated into the daily patterns of life in schools. Many approaches and strategies are in use that establish these processes. A missing link in many such efforts is a constructivist necessity: to begin our enquiries by evoking our previous experiences, assumptions, values and beliefs about the issues at hand. Doing this makes it more likely that we will be able to pose relevant questions and mediate new learnings.

One of the most comprehensive enquiry approaches is what is known as whole school collaborative action research. It is 'comprehensive' in that it aims at whole school improvement while building collaborative enquiry habits of mind. In addition to action research, the following strategies are effective in building a culture of enquiry:

- Work sessions for examining and assessing pupil work.
- Peer coaching and peer review.
- Collective problem-solving strategies that include problem finding, posing alternative actions, monitoring and evaluation.
- Other forms of research such as reviews of the literature, internet searches and chat rooms, visiting other schools, and attending network meetings and conferences.
- Examination of disaggregated data (breaking down performance data by gender, race, Special Educational Needs (SES), ethnicity, disabilities) and such other readily available school data as attendance, suspensions, expulsions, standardized scores.
- Grounding of your work in the school's vision but continually comparing practice and results with intentions. 'Is this what we planned?', 'Are we achieving what we had hoped?', 'Are our children learning to read?'

Each of these strategies has its own strengths. Choices are guided by the questions you have to answer, your priorities, the roles and structures that you've established and the skilfulness of the teachers. Some of these strategies should be initially undertaken with technical assistance.

Organize the school for leadership work

To organize for the leadership work described above means to establish structures, groups and roles that serve as the infrastructure for the self-renewing processes of a culture of enquiry. The selection of groups will be informed by the key issues or questions to hand. Questions to consider when designing school structures include:

- How will we make decisions at our school?
- How will we organize for reflection, enquiry, dialogue and action?
- How will we maximize involvement and interaction?
- How will the groups relate to each other?
- What forms of communication will create dense feedback loops among groups and individuals?
- How will the roles of group participants be described?
- What groups or individuals will participate in professional networks? How will ideas from those sources stimulate and inform the work within the school?
- How will we provide a forum for feedback to and from other schools, organizations and universities?

Answers to these guiding questions will focus the planning for school organization. Schools have found many working arrangements useful: leadership teams, facilitation teams or research teams (for guiding action research), ad hoc groups on various topics: school climate, assessment task force, interdisciplinary teams, school improvement groups, among others.

Roles and responsibilities will emerge and be defined in reference to these structures and the purposes they serve. For instance, as teachers begin to view themselves as leaders, they will also take on the responsibility of mentor, facilitator, coach and mediator. University personnel, LEA or other school personnel, retired educators, or community members from other professions can be valued members of any of these groups. These partners can provide technical assistance; serve as a coach, mediator or critical friend; or just offer an alternative perspective.

Generate purposeful collaboration

If sustained improvement is to be achieved, teacher part-nerships and other forms of purposeful collaboration should be encouraged. This implies a form of professional development and learning that is premised on collabor-ation, co-operation and networking. It implies a view of the school as a learning community where teachers and students learn together. The importance of teacher devel-opment within school improvement has long been estab-lished. It is also clear that teachers develop through enquiry into and reflection on their own practice. Schools that are failing tend to be characterized by an impover-ishment in teaching and teacher development. They are schools where there is a culture of individualism and where the process of teaching is rarely evaluated or discussed.

Evidence would suggest that those schools engaged in improvement activities build communities that are col-laborative and empowering. They foster positive relation-ships and allow all voices to be heard and acknowledged. In this sense, school improvement means moving from a culture of individualism to what Clarke (2002; 3) calls 'a renewed sense of social responsibility.'

Implement your plans for building leadership capacity

Many leaders in the field of educational reform have helped us to recognize the developmental nature of implementation. This is particularly true in building leadership capacity, since the changes at hand are both personal and organizational. Educators, parents and pupils are often required to alter their self-perceptions in order to perceive themselves as leaders. Redefining leadership can help tremendously. These changing self-perceptions are necessarily accompanied by a redesigned pattern of organization for the school and LEA that allows for the work of leadership to be carried out. This is difficult work, requiring persistence, patience and deeply held beliefs about the capabilities of individuals and schools.

Persistence is hanging in there until the work is done, but it is a particular way of 'hanging in there'. Persistence does not mean patiently waiting for people to 'see the light'. Rather, it entails listening, posing tough questions, describing, mediating, and surfacing and confronting conflict. When opposition occurs in the form of active resistance or passive aggressiveness, it is vital to ask about the source of the feelings, listen carefully and enter into dialogue about the implications of these conflicting ideas. It is not useful to do a 'hard sell'. What is vital is to secure agreement to stay in the dialogue.

Since the work of building leadership capacity, like any important endeavour, is developmental, there will be indicators of progress at different stages of the journey. A few indicators that will tell you that you are making progress are:

- listening to each other and building on each other's ideas
- posing essential questions, the answers to which will address the school's fundamental purpose
- challenging and mediating resistance
- encountering and solving problems – rather than only describing difficult conditions
- visiting each other's classrooms and reflecting with each other on what you observe
- transforming cynicism into hopefulness by transforming the school's most challenging issues into clear statements of purpose or enquiry
- talking about teaching and learning in the staff room
- initiating innovative ideas.

For more indicators of progress, see columns 3 and 4 in

the Rubric of emerging teacher leadership in appendix B. Remember, leadership capacity is basically content free; that is, it is the fundamental work of schooling that accompanies any reform effort – improving literacy, instruction, assessment, school restructuring, parent involvement. To implement any innovation and pursue school improvement successfully requires strengthening the leadership capacity of the school.

Build a professional learning community

In order to improve and to sustain improvement over time schools need to build and nurture a sense of a professional learning community. In the most effective schools, there is evidence of positive relationships both within and outside the school. Barth (1990: 45) describes a professional learning community as one where adults and students learn, and each energises and contributes to the learning of the other. A professional learning community is one in which there are shared norms and values among teachers and students. These norms and values represent the fundamental beliefs of those within the community and become the defining purpose of the school.

To build a professional learning community requires schools to consider the type of school culture that prevails and to seek ways of changing it for the better. Learning within an organization is optimal in an environment of shared leadership and shared power. To foster such an environment requires teamwork, collaboration and a commitment to enquiry. Connections are particularly important in building community. As Sergiovanni (2001: 63) notes 'community is something most of us want in order to experience the sense and meaning that we need in our lives. We cannot go it alone. We have to be connected somehow, somewhere.' Community is a particularly important source of connection for children and young people. If the needs of students to belong are not met by the school then they will find it outside the school.

In schools that are improving there are shared norms, shared values, agreed goals and common aspirations. These are schools where the social relations are functional and where trust and respect are at the core of all developmental work. This does not occur by chance but results from the deliberate effort of staff and students to communicate and to collaborate with each other. Sergiovanni (2001) notes that such communities of responsibility are far from easy to cultivate but are necessary to generate and sustain school improvement over time. Further insights into creating professional learning communities can be found in Chapter 9.

Conditions and assumptions as the basis for building leadership capacity

In Chapter 1, we described five leadership assumptions that serve as the basic premises for building leadership capacity in schools and LEAs. They are:

1 Leadership is not trait theory; leadership and leader are not the same.
2 Leadership is about learning.
3 Everyone has the potential and right to work as a leader.
4 Leading is a shared endeavour.
5 Leadership requires the redistribution of power and authority.

These assumptions provide the conceptual framework for establishing the conditions described in this chapter:

1 Get to know each other.
2 Assess teachers and school capacity for leadership.
3 Develop a culture of enquiry.
4 Generate purposeful collaboration.
5 Organize the school community for leadership work.
6 Implement your plans for building leadership capacity.
7 Build a learning community.

Establishing these seven conditions and focusing on the

five assumptions will build leadership capacity in your school.

Reflect for a moment . . .

- How far are these seven conditions apparent in your school?
- What, if anything, is missing?
- What needs to be done?
- Who can help?
- What types of internal and external agency do we need?

Building leadership capacity in schools is reliant on both internal agency and external agency. Internal agency incorporates the actions and leadership activities of teachers and pupils. External agency incorporates the actions and leadership activites of the wider community and the LEA. The next chapter considers the role of the LEA as an external agent on building leadership capacity.

8 BUILDING LEADERSHIP CAPACITY FOR SCHOOL IMPROVEMENT: THE ROLE OF THE LEA

> The world within which individual teachers and students live and move does matter. Other people and other agencies do matter.
>
> (Mitchell and Sackney 2000: 4)

In judging a school's ability to build leadership capacity for improvement, one of the key questions must be 'how near are we to being a professional learning community?' In other words, how close is the school to becoming an improving school? Schools differ considerably in size, culture, type and context but the research evidence shows that levels of effectiveness and improvement are not fixed but can be modified by a combination of internal and external agency. As seen in Chapter 7, internal agency can be generated through empowering teachers to lead and to take responsibility for school development. Building internal leadership capacity enhances the possibility of sustaining school improvement over time. But where does external agency come from? What is the role of the external change agent in building leadership capacity for school improvement?

While schools can and do improve themselves, this is rarely achieved without effective support from outside. External agency has been shown to be a prerequisite of successful school improvement. In the majority of cases, this external agency is provided by the Local Education Authority (LEA) and there is increasing evidence of the importance of the LEA in school improvement (Harris 2001). It is clear many schools that find themselves in 'Special Measures' or 'Serious Weaknesses' have not been solely responsible for their fate. Evidence would suggest that weak LEA support is a contributory factor to schools spiralling towards failure. Clearly, it is not the only variable but it is more difficult to improve a school within an LEA that is itself struggling to provide adequate support and guidance. As Lambert (2002) suggests, 'we cannot save education one school at a time' and this highlights the need to look carefully at the provision of LEA services to schools. In the best LEAs the weakest schools will survive and possibly thrive. By contrast in the poorer LEAs, the better schools are in danger of imploding over time. Hence, LEAs are important partners in the pursuit of sustained school improvement. They have a particular contribution to make and can vary quite considerably in effectiveness.

The LEAs can support schools in building leadership capacity for improvement in four important ways:

1 **Contextualizing school improvement** – the LEA has an important role to play in providing schools with a framework for improvement that takes account of individual school context. The LEA is well placed to understand the individual demands and needs of different schools. Consequently, LEA advisers can ensure that

school improvement is approached in a way that addresses the particular needs of individual schools.

2 **Developing a bias for action** – in the initial stages of school improvement, schools can spend a large amount of time planning with little emphasis on action. It is important therefore, that some external pressure is exerted to encourage them to put their plans into action. There is evidence to suggest that the LEA adviser can influence schools to move towards action and can assist them to develop a bias for action that will lead to successful innovation and development.

3 **Linking school development to local and national priorities** – schools that are improving have been shown to match internal development needs to external demands or priorities. External, and sometimes competing, demands arise from local and national priorities. The LEA is in a position to provide schools with a broader perspective on these competing priorities and ensure that school level developments reflect and, where possible, complement the developmental imperatives at the local and national levels.

4 **Maintaining momentum** – within any school improvement project a major challenge for schools is to maintain the momentum for innovation and development. There is a tendency for well-intentioned change to be lost at the point of implementation and for improvement efforts to lose momentum over time. A key role for the LEA, therefore, is to monitor the progress of innovations and developments within individual schools and to provide pressure and support where progress seems to be slow.

Unlike other external change agents, LEA advisers have a close and intimate knowledge of their schools. Consequently, they are able to adopt a distinctive interventionist stance and to work more regularly and closely with schools.

Think about your LEA . . .

- How far is it supportive of your school improvement efforts?
- How effective is it in supporting schools?
- How might your school more effectively use the LEA as an external change agent?

Positive LEA relationships with schools involve two correlates that maximize reciprocity. The first is high engagement – this means frequent interaction and two-way communication. The second is low bureaucratization – this means the absence of extensive rules, regulations and excessive 'red tape'. It is important that LEA policies promote high engagement rather than bureaucratization. If schools are to look towards the LEA for support and guidance they will need to be convinced that the LEA can 'add significant value' to their school improvement efforts. Some of this 'added value' will be provided through professional development opportunities while some will be found in the skills, abilities and experience of advisers to assist in the process of school improvement.

The stages of change: generating school improvement

The process of change for school improvement has been broadly categorized into three phases by Fullan (1999). Phase one is the 'initiation stage' where schools are commencing work and seeking a focus for their improvement work. Phase two is the 'implementation stage' where schools are putting their improvement plans into action. Phase three is the 'maintaining and sustaining' phase where the process and practice of school improvement becomes an integral part of school development. At each of these phases, different types of external agency are required to match the particular developmental needs of the school.

At the outset, schools will be seeking to establish a developmental focus for their improvement work. While some schools might be very clear about the direction of their improvement efforts, others will need assistance and guidance. The LEA adviser is well placed to provide such support and is able to assist schools in diagnosing their strengths and weaknesses. This is achieved through the provision of data analysis and critical friendship. At the LEA level, a great deal of data is collected and generated relating to the performance of individual schools. LEAs and schools are in receipt of a wide range of data of a comparative nature concerning a school's effectiveness. Often, this data is not presented in a way that is accessible or easily interpreted by schools. Consequently, the LEA can assist schools in understanding and using this data for improvement purposes. The analysis of data by schools is an important means of self-evaluation and can assist schools in focusing on the most important issues or areas for change.

Once schools have formulated their improvement plan, they subsequently move into the implementation phase. This requires them to instigate change and to commence their improvement activities. It is widely acknowledged that during this phase schools require a great deal of support to implement change successfully. The LEA therefore, has an important role to play in providing the practical, technical and emotional support needed by various schools at this critical stage. This support includes staff development and offering evaluative feedback.

Within any school improvement activity the provision of training and support for staff is essential. The LEA offers an important source of training and development. In many cases, this training is provided in direct response to a particular set of school needs or addresses the specific needs of a group of staff within a school. LEA personnel can respond more quickly to requests for additional support from schools than other external agents. LEA advisers are more able to provide follow-up visits and ongoing support that builds on the training provision. They also provide important evaluative feedback to schools that allows them to take stock of progress with their innovation or development work.

Within successful school improvement, teachers are encouraged to build their own professional communities both within and outside the school. LEA personnel play a central role in establishing professional networks or communities through their work with schools. They provide additional professional development opportunities and use their local knowledge to establish links between schools for support and developmental purposes. LEA advisers also have mechanisms for sharing and disseminating good practice.

Schools that build capacity for improvement are those which use their links with other schools to maximum advantage (Harris 2002a). The networks established and facilitated by the LEA have been shown to provide schools with important opportunities to learn from each other and to solve problems collectively. These professional communities have been shown to be highly influential in enabling schools to move forward and instrumental in sustaining school improvement. There is increasing evidence to suggest that the external agency provided by the LEA advisers is a crucial component of successful school improvement. Where this is not provided or where provision is limited, the progress made by schools has been shown to be significantly less than in schools where such LEA support is in place.

To summarize, there are four discernible and discrete dimensions of the LEAs role as an external change agent.

1 The LEA can help *translate* the principles of school improvement into the policies of senior staff and into the practices of individual classrooms. This bridging or brokering function remains a central responsibility for the adviser. It ensures that links both within and between individual schools are secure and that opportunities for meaningful development are maximized.

2 The LEA helps staff to develop *ownership* of a particular change or development. This role in shaping and sharing the school's vision for improvement is a form of

leadership that is participative and tranformative. The LEAs can use 'power with' and 'power through' to assist staff to cohere around a particular development and to foster a more collaborative way of working. They work with senior managers and teachers to shape school improvement efforts and take some lead in guiding staff towards a collective end.

3 LEA advisers address individual staff and school *performance*. At a macro level this involves monitoring attainment, assessing performance and setting clear targets. At the micro level it suggests an important coaching or mentoring role as LEA advisers work with teachers to improve the quality of teaching and learning.

4 The liaison or representative role of the LEA: LEAs are links to the external environment and are important sources of *expertise* and information. They have a particular responsibility for school performance and improvement and are therefore able to draw on additional resource and expertise if required.

The success of the LEA in school improvement resides in the fact that LEA advisers have a close relationship with schools and that they understand the context in which they operate. They act as critical friends and offer much needed encouragement and emotional support as schools embark on and manage the process of change. In LEAs where there is an emphasis on compliance and standardization rather than on professional development and system-wide coherence, the possibility of an LEA contributing to school improvement is dramatically reduced.

The major purpose of developing leadership capacity is to create the internal conditions to sustain improvement. It takes a reciprocal relationship between the LEA and the school to create the conditions where sustainability is a possibility. It takes an understanding of the need for shared leadership within the school and the aspiration that schools should be places of learning for teacher and pupils. The most effective LEAs accept the importance of generating leadership at all levels within the school and investing in community learning. They are the LEAs that have vision and encourage broad-based skilful involvement in the work of leadership.

Reflect for a moment . . .

- To what extent is your LEA encouraging broad-based skilful involvement in the work of leadership at your school?
- What feedback could you give to your LEA to ensure your school receives the support it needs?

As we saw from the three case studies, where teachers are empowered to lead the potential exists to alter the cultural context in which teachers teach and students learn for the better. Essentially, schools that are improving build leadership capacity and invest in meaningful professional development. The next chapter considers the role of professional development in school improvement.

9 BUILDING LEADERSHIP

CAPACITY FOR SCHOOL

IMPROVEMENT: THE ROLE

OF PROFESSIONAL

DEVELOPMENT

Professional learning communities hold the key to transformation – the kind that has real effects on people's lives.

(Wenger 1998: 85)

Throughout this book there has been an emphasis on the centrality of the role of the teacher in the pursuit of school improvement. It has been emphasized that teacher leadership and teacher development is the key to building the capacity for sustained school improvement. The evidence points to the importance of teachers working together and learning together in generating the capacity for change. It emphasises that to be a Quadrant 4 school i.e. a professional learning community investment needs to be made in building leadership skills and capability. However, while teacher collaboration may be highly desirable it is not always easy to achieve in practice. In many ways the design and organization of schools presents the biggest challenge to teacher collaboration and the building of learning communities. The fragmented and individualized ways of working that characterized Rookwood and Manor are largely a function of the physical, structural and organizational constraints that exist within those schools. Teachers who do want to work together often find the barriers of time, competing tasks and physical geography difficult to overcome. This implies a deliberate and radical shift in the way schools are organized, if meaningful teacher collaboration is to flourish and grow.

Schools that improve and continue to improve, invest in the life of the school as a 'learning organization' where members are constantly striving to seek new ways of improving their practice (Senge 1990). An optimal school learning environment provides teachers with opportunities to work and learn together. It promotes sharing ideas and the open exchange of opinions and experiences. Teacher collaboration, reflection, enquiry and partnership are ways of building capacity for school improvement. This is something that teachers can and should actively create themselves. Constructing and participating in the building of professional communities in schools is by its nature a vibrant form of professional development.

If the use of new practices is to be sustained and changes are to endure, regular opportunities for teachers to share perspectives and seek solutions will be required. Working collaboratively not only reduces the sense of isolation many teachers feel but also enhances the quality of the work produced. Working as part of a professional development community helps focus attention on shared purpose and the goals that lead to school improvement.

Professional development is continuous learning focused on the central goal of making a difference in the lives of diverse students. It is the sum total of formal and informal learning pursued and experienced by the teacher in a compelling learning environment under conditions of complexity and dynamic change.

If schools are serious about building the leadership capacity for school improvement, then teacher development in that process should be a driving force. For improvement to take place all stakeholders need to be involved and engaged. In schools that are improving, such as Highfields School, a distinctive feature is how far they work together. In schools that have built leadership capacity, a climate of collaboration exists and there is a collective commitment to work together. This climate is not simply given but is the result of discussion, development and dialogue among those working within the organization.

A school that has built leadership capacity consists of teachers who are active in constructing meaning and collaborating in mutual enquiry and learning. It is also a learning community where the learning of teachers receives the same attention as the learning of students. In Highfields School, for example, the teachers and pupils shared decision making, innovation and implementation of new ideas. They worked collaboratively to create learning opportunities and created avenues for development and change. Highfields School is primarily about people, the way they interact and learn from each other. At the core of the learning community at Highfields is collaborative practice and shared enquiry.

Meaningful professional development

Much more is now known about the conditions under which teachers develop to the benefit of themselves and their pupils. The problem remaining is *how* to build learning communities within schools for teachers and pupils. These do not occur naturally. In many schools the norms of practice are not those of collaboration or mutual sharing but tend to be isolation or 'balkanization'. In Manor Primary School, for example, teachers are isolated and rarely work together. In this school, strategies for powerful change are required that engage teachers in meaningful professional development. While it is recognized that teachers' needs will vary according to circumstance, personal and professional histories and current dispositions, the matching of appropriate professional development provision to particular professional needs is essential if effective learning is to take place. This 'fit' between the developmental needs of the teacher and the selected activity is critically important in ensuring that there is a positive impact at the school and classroom level.

Where professional development opportunities are insensitive to the concerns of individual participants, and make little effort to relate learning experiences to workplace conditions, they make little impact on teachers or their pupils. Building leadership capacity requires a constructivist approach to learning where teachers learn together and construct meaning from interaction, discussion and professional dialogue. Research has shown that in order to achieve improvements in teaching and better learning outcomes for students, teachers need to be engaged in meaningful professional development that promotes enquiry, creativity and innovation. Improvements in teaching are most likely to occur where there are opportunities for teachers to work together and to learn from each other. As evidenced at Rookwood Comprehensive School, working with colleagues dispelled feelings of professional isolation and assisted in enhancing teachers' classroom practices. At Highfields, the collaboration among teachers strengthened resolve, permitted vulnerabilities and carried people through the frustrations that accompany change in its early stages. It also eliminated the possibility of duplication and allowed greater co-ordination and consistency of teaching approaches.

Collaboration

As noted earlier, leadership processes must enable participants to engage in a shared sense of purpose – a purpose
made real by the collaboration of committed adults. Collaboration improves the quality of student learning by
improving the quality of teaching. It encourages risk taking, greater diversity in teaching methods and an
improved sense of efficacy among teachers. Teachers are
more able to implement new ideas within the context of
supportive collaborative relationships or partnerships. By
working collaboratively teachers are able to consider the
different ways in which the subject matter can be taught.
Collaboration leads to a pooling of the collected knowledge, expertise and capacities of teachers within the subject area. It increases teachers' opportunities to learn from
each other between classrooms, between subject areas and
between schools. The insulated and often segregated
departments of secondary schools make it difficult for
teachers to learn from each other. Consequently, schools
need to build a climate of collaboration premised on
communication, sharing and opportunities for teachers to
work together. Collaboration is important because it creates a collective professional confidence that allow
teachers to interact more confidently and assertively.

As highlighted earlier in the book, the leadership skills
needed for collaborative work involve the ability to:

● develop a shared sense of purpose with colleagues
● facilitate group processes
● communicate well
● understand transition and change and their effects on
  each other
● mediate conflict
● develop positive relationships.

Collaboration improves the quality of student learning
by improving the quality of teaching. It encourages risk
taking, greater diversity in teaching methods and an
improved sense of efficacy among teachers. The principle

of teacher collaboration is at the core of constructing a positive working community and is consistently listed in the
effective schools' literature as correlating positively with
student outcomes. Collaboration is important because it
creates a collective professional confidence that allow
teachers to interact more confidently and assertively. The
insulated and often segregated departments of secondary
schools make it difficult for teachers to learn from each
other. Consequently, schools need to build a climate
of collaboration within, premised on communication,
sharing and opportunities for teachers to work together.

For collaboration to influence professional growth and
development it has to be premised on mutual enquiry and
sharing. There is sufficient evaluative evidence to show
that when teachers are engaged in dialogue with each
other about their practice then meaningful reflection and
teacher learning occurs. As teachers search for new understanding or knowledge with other teachers, the possibility
and potential for school improvement is significantly
increased. The school, as a learning community, is nur-
tured and sustained when individuals reflect on, assess
and discuss professional practice. Building the capacity for
school improvement necessitates paying careful attention
to how collaborative processes in schools are fostered and
developed. Where teachers feel confident in their own
leadership capacity, in the leadership capacity of their colleagues and in the capacity of the school to promote professional development, school improvement is more
likely to occur.

Reflection and enquiry

Reflection leads to the opportunity to 'run with' an idea,
to see it through. If ideas are customarily blocked by the
head, ideas are not likely to blossom on a regular basis. If a
school community feels that an idea warrants a trial,
many doors need to be opened to enable those teacher
leaders (entrepreneurs) to transform the idea into reality.

Innovators should be encouraged to involve other colleagues, to establish responsible criteria for success, and
to create a realistic timeline for monitoring and evaluation.

Those teachers who recognize that enquiry and reflection are important processes in the classroom find it easier
to sustain an improvement effort around teaching and
learning practices. The reflective teacher is one who turns
attention to the immediate reality of classroom practice.
Reflection is centrally concerned with improving practice
rather than collecting knowledge. As each school, subject
area and classroom are unique, reflective teachers develop
their practice through engaging in enquiry and critical
analysis of their teaching and the teaching of others. In
order for teachers to be reflective about their practice
there has to be 'a feedback loop', a means by which they
can consider their work in a critical way.

One powerful way in which teachers are encouraged to
reflect on and improve their practice is through a process
of enquiry. As illustrated by the cadre group at Highfields
School, collaboration in dialogue and action can provide
sources of feedback and comparison that prompt teachers
to reflect on their own practice. Engaging teachers in the
process of 'systematic enquiry' does not necessarily mean
a detailed knowledge of research but rather involvement
in a form of systematic reflection on practice. The argument for research as a basis for teaching rests on two main
principles. First, that teacher research is linked to the
strengthening of teacher judgement and consequently to
the self-directed improvement of practice. Second, that
the most important focus for research is the curriculum in
that it is the medium through which the communication
of knowledge in schools takes place.

Action enquiry is essentially practical and applied. It is
driven by the need for teachers to solve practical, real
world problems. The research needs to be undertaken as
part of teachers' practice rather than a bolt-on extra.
Action research and enquiry is concerned with practical
issues that arise naturally as part of professional activity.
This practical orientation is one of the reasons why action

enquiry remains a popular form of research activity among teachers. For teachers, values such as empowerment of learners and respect for students' views may be at the centre of their action enquiry activities. Improving practice is about realizing such values and necessarily involves a continuing process of reflection on the part of the teachers. However, the kind of reflection encouraged by the action enquiry process is quite distinctive from an ends-driven type of reasoning. The reflection is about choosing a course of action, or a particular set of circumstances based on a set of values or principles. Action enquiry improves practice by developing the teacher's capacity to make judgements about their own practice.

Professional development and improvement

Schools that improve and continue to improve, invest in the life of the school as a learning community where members are constantly striving to seek new ways of improving their practice. An optimal school learning environment provides teachers with opportunities to work and learn together. It promotes sharing ideas and the open exchange of opinions and experiences. Teacher collaboration, reflection, enquiry and partnership are ways of building a professional development community. This is something that teachers can and should actively create themselves. Constructing and participating in the building of professional communities in schools is by its nature a vibrant form of teacher and school development.

Professional development is continuous learning focused on the central goal of making a difference in the lives of diverse students. It is the sum total of formal and informal learning pursued and experienced by the teacher in a compelling learning environment under conditions of complexity and dynamic change. If the use of new practices is to be sustained and changes are to endure, regular opportunities for teachers to share perspectives and seek solutions will be required. Working collaboratively not only reduces the sense of isolation many teachers feel but also enhances the quality of the work produced. Working as part of a professional development community helps focus attention on shared purpose and the goals that lead to school improvement.

There are a number of important messages about the role of professional development in building leadership capacity for school improvement:

- it is important to foster *deep collaboration* and not superficial co-operation among the teaching staff
- it is important to form *partnerships* within schools and to network with other schools and agencies
- it is important to generate *teacher leadership and pupil leadership*
- it is important to provide opportunities for teacher *enquiry and action research*
- it is important to allocate time for personal reflection and opportunities for teachers to talk together about *teaching and learning*
- it is important to generate the *collective capability*; expertise and commitment of teachers is one way of ensuring that all teachers are involved.

Pause for thought . . .

- How far has your school built the capacity for improvement?
- What needs to happen in the short, medium and long term?
- What needs to happen immediately?

If you are serious about building the capacity for improvement in your school, then the centrality of community involvement in that process is critical. All stakeholders need to be involved and engaged. Schools that improve provide a context for collaboration and the generation of shared meaning. Schools that build leadership capacity hold the key to transformation – they can make a real and sustained difference to the achievement of young people. They ensure that irrespective of context, circumstance or political imperatives they are able to affect the lives of all young people, for the better.

A final question: Schools that build the capacity for improvement invest in teachers and their professional development. How could professional development be improved and enhanced in your school?

This book has attempted to introduce some ideas about leadership, capacity building and change that will be new for some of you and for others simply offer a consolidation or extension of what you already knew. We recognize that individual queries, questions and issues raised by reading this book are inevitable. Consequently, in the next chapter we try to anticipate some of the areas that might require further clarification and provide some answers to your questions.

PART 4

CAPACITY BUILDING

IN ACTION

10 SOME QUESTIONS

AND A FEW ANSWERS

This chapter aims to anticipate and answer some of your questions about building leadership capacity for school improvement. Many of these questions have been asked in workshops, classes and conferences. Hopefully, you will find some of your questions answered here.

Once again, what is meant by leadership capacity?

Leadership capacity refers to broad-based, skilful involvement in the work of leadership. The work of leadership involves attention to shared learning leading to shared purpose and action. In schools, increased leadership capacity means that the head is one leader – and a very important leader – but he or she does not fill all or even most of the leadership roles in the building.

How is leadership capacity different from shared decision making?

Shared decision making is one aspect of leadership capacity, but learning in schools is about more than decisions. It is about our daily work together – reflection, dialogue, enquiry and action. This work involves new roles and responsibilities that reframe all of our inter-actions together, not just those at decision points.

You've chosen five critical features of leadership capacity. Why these five?

These five features (broad-based skilful involvement; enquiry-based use of information to inform decisions and practice; roles and responsibilities reflect broad involve-ment and collaboration; reflective practice/innovation is the norm; high pupil achievement) are firmly tied to school improvement and pupil achievement. You may have recognized that the fifth feature, high pupil achievement, is both a dimension of collaborative work (teaching and learning for children) and an outcome. Together, these features form a dynamic relationship; no one or two features will result in high leadership capacity or high pupil achievement. It is a case of the sum being greater than the parts.

Is it the goal that every educator become a leader? If so, why?

Yes. Leaders are perceived as consummate learners who attend to the learning of both adults and children – includ-ing themselves, of course. This is what it should mean to be a professional educator. That does not mean that all leadership work will look the same. While some educators will chair committees and facilitate large group meetings, others will focus their energies on implementing peer coaching, team teaching, conducting collaborative action research and demonstrating reflective practice.

There are those teachers who do not see themselves as leaders – and do not want to see themselves as leaders. How do I work with them?

By redefining leadership as constructivist learning, teachers are more able to find this work congruent with their work with children. Some teachers will take on several leadership roles; others may wish to accept fewer or more modest roles or tasks. In a setting that encourages leadership, it is a rare teacher who will entirely resist this opportunity.

Why do you insist on using the therapeutic term 'co-dependency' in reference to relationships in school?
Co-dependency refers to dependence on each other to reinforce archaic roles and uses of power and authority. It is an apt term for the entangled, traditional relationships in schools that have kept educators from growing. Without broad-based leadership, the ability of a school to grow and become better for children is limited.

Is there a tension between enquiry and innovation?
Yes, there is such a tension. Genuine enquiry tends to produce home-grown solutions. Innovation has sometimes meant finding a good programme elsewhere and inserting it into the school. Best practices that have been carefully researched can be very useful to a school. When enquiry leads a school to realize what is needed, a survey of promising practices can produce a programme that is well suited for the school. Broad leadership allows the administration and subject to blend, adapt and adjust practices to fit that particular school.

Our school is considered successful, yet certain groups of pupils are doing poorly. Where do we start?
You start by having a thoughtful dialogue among school community members (including parents) in order to understand the condition. This dialogue needs to consider the disaggregated data that led to the conclusion that particular groups of pupils were not doing well. Participants will need to confront their own assumptions about which groups of pupils can learn and under what circumstances they learn best. The next step is to assign the practical tasks that need to be accomplished to make the school truly successful.

How does all of this fit in with the movement towards a standards-driven system?

As we have noted, leadership capacity is an essential element of any reform. The key issue with standards-driven system is how the standards were devised and who decides how they are to be implemented. Standards that are collaboratively designed and implemented by using (1) the expert knowledge of school teachers and community members and (2) the findings of best practice can evoke commitment and competence from all concerned. Even if the standards are externally imposed, teachers can determine how they will be applied or adapted in their school's particular situation.

Why are changing roles so central to the work of building leadership capacity?

Changing roles grow out of changing self-perceptions; and, in turn, new roles provide 'spaces' in which individuals can redefine what it is to be a teacher, parent, pupil, administrator. New roles are accompanied by new responsibilities. As roles evolve, members of a school community reach a point of collective responsibility – a condition demonstrably linked to high pupil achievement.

What do you mean by responsibility?

We prefer the term 'responsibility' to 'accountability'. Responsibility involves an internal commitment to self-improvement, the improvement of others around us, and the school community at large. Accountability, on the other hand, has tended to mean that we are being 'held accountable' by some outside authority. Accountability measures often mitigate against the development of responsibility, since external demands can evoke compliance and resistance.

You've given a lot of attention to communication and information systems. Schools are closely knit places; can't we just talk with each other?

'Talking with each other' is often random, erratic and

personality-dependent. An information and feedback system needs to be consciously planned and implemented in order to involve everyone with similar frequency and quality. 'Quality' here refers to respectful listening, asking essential questions, giving and receiving specific feedback.

I think I'm an effective teacher (and my head and colleagues seem to agree), but I work best by myself. How will I fit into the 'new order'?
Adults, like children, have different preferred learning styles. It is important that learning alternatives exist that take account of all styles. However, it is also important that adults work to expand their learning style repertoire in order to engage with all learners collectively. Part of the reason that we recommend results-orientated conversations is to attend to the frustration felt by some adults when they are caught up in open-ended discussions and conversations. As stated earlier, some teachers will accept more leadership responsibilities than others – and no teacher should be coerced into a role that makes him or her very uncomfortable.

With all of this involvement in the work of leading, isn't the classroom being neglected?
Since pupil achievement is firmly connected to the adult learning and leading behaviours recommended here, building leadership capacity is not a diversion but a necessity. It is also important to remember that there are two forms of expanding leadership roles: taking on additional tasks or functions and behaving more skilfully in daily interactions (that is, asking questions, listening, provoking, giving feedback). The latter form doesn't take more time; it merely reframes how we do what we already do.

Isn't there a danger in so much involvement outside the school?
Well, yes. But there is a greater danger from too little

involvement outside the school. Schools need to help create congruent contexts ('user-friendly' communities and LEAs) in which to function, broader feedback loops for self-renewal, and opportunities for professional development. Isolated school environments contribute to ingrown, self-indulgent solutions. As educators develop, they naturally assume more responsibility for the broader community and the profession. Such expanding responsibilities will not occur if outside opportunities do not exist for each subject member.

If you work in a LEA that says to the head, 'The buck stops at your desk', do we have a chance at building high leadership capacity?

When a narrow, hierarchical approach to accountability is used, the work before you is much more difficult. An LEA needs to change its accountability system from being person-dependent to being school community-dependent. The establishment of a broad-based enquiry system at each site that will build in both self-evaluation and self-renewal is vital and complex. Yet, as we have seen in the Highfields School story, a school can go a long way towards shared responsibility if the head is willing to make new roles and responsibilities explicit to all concerned.

Aren't you underplaying the role of the head?

On the surface, it may seem that way. Actually, as noted in Chapter 2, the role of the head in building leadership capacity is more demanding and complex than the old work of telling and directing. However, the head now shares the spotlight with teachers, parents, pupils and other community members – more a choreographer than a prima ballerina.

What are the LEA policies critical for building leadership capacity?

Policies need to be continually reviewed to make sure they are truly supportive of the teaching programme in classsrooms and schools. Some guidelines for analysing and testing policies appear in the appendices. Underlying these guidelines is the conviction that, like schools, LEAs themselves must become constructivist learning communities – using, promoting and facilitating the reciprocal processes that are advocated for schools.

With broad-based leadership and collective responsibility, aren't heads losing control?

Yes, they are losing one form of control – the form that stifles development. A new form of 'control' emerges, one that invests itself in learning and long-range results. These new forms require that heads and other members of the senior management team let go of the need for daily predictabilities and narrow objectives. They continue to provide oversight, they are even more involved in the life of the school but they resist the temptation to impose quick change through top-down mandates and fiats.

This seems all too complicated. Can ordinary teachers be teacher leaders?

Never underestimate the capacity of people to understand and use ideas that are congruent with their desire for learning.

If we all take these ideas to heart and implement them, how soon will we have improving schools?

If you focus your attention on building leadership capacity in schools, within 18 months you will notice major dispositional shifts among almost all involved. By the second year major structural changes will be in place. And, by the end of the second year, you should notice changes in pupil academic performance (improvements in social behaviour will come earlier). Since the educational lore is that it takes three to ten years to improve a school, building leadership capacity with constructivist strategies can be surprisingly efficient!

What can help my school become a Quadrant 4 school i.e. a professional learning community?

The National College for School Leadership (NCSL) offers a programme designed to improve learning opportunities for pupils and to support the development of schools as professional learning communities. It places teachers, leaders and schools at the heart of innovation and know-ledge creation within the profession, and enables the development of local, context-specific practices and solutions that can be explained and interpreted by schools in other contexts – at the heart of knowledge networks. Networked Learning Communities (NLCs) will act as critical friends to one another and each will additionally elect to have an external partner, which may include Higher Education Institutions (HEIs), Local Education Authorities (LEAs) or Community Groups.

This is a design-based innovation. Learning networks are being promoted to enrich professional practice as they create and transfer knowledge to support improvements in teaching, learning and organizational restructuring. In achieving this goal, schools within NLCs will:

- Collaborate around the study of teaching and learning – within and between schools.
- Promote and recognize practitioner enquiry – creating knowledge together.
- Engage with and learn from theory and research generated by involvement in the enquiry process to build the knowledge base about what works.
- Develop and utilize a wide variety of approaches to Continuing Professional Development (CPD) including: coaching, mentoring, induction programmes, shadowing and internal and external programmes of learning that qualify for accreditation.

For more information about Networked Learning Communities go to www.ncsl.org.uk

FINAL WORD

> Rare is the effective school that does not have an effective head. Adding teacher leadership to the equation ensures that school improvement becomes a way of life in the school.
>
> (Sergiovanni 2001: 16)

While building the leadership capacity for school improvement may be desirable, it is not without its challenges. Building leadership capacity implies a different power relationship within the school where the distinctions between followers and leaders blur. As we have seen throughout this book, building leadership capacity overturns the 'status quo' of leader and led. It confronts the limitations of 'top-down' reform, pointing instead to teachers as instigators and agents of change. It questions the wisdom of investing in the leadership development of individuals and opens up the possibility for all teachers to become leaders at various times. Building leadership capacity implies a redistribution of power and a re-alignment of authority within the school as an organization. It suggests that leadership is a shared and collective endeavour that should engage *all* teachers within the school. It also implies that the context in which people work and learn together is where they construct and refine meaning leading to a shared purpose or set of goals.

Building leadership capacity asks those within schools to step out of the 'comfort zone' and do things differently. Inevitably, there will be those in schools who will resist this through fear, vulnerability or a sheer indifference to improvement or change. The desire to stay safe is often more powerful than the excitement of change or risk taking. But we know that all schools have the potential to improve and that teachers have a key role to play in sustaining school improvement. Although the idea of 'teacher leadership' is still relatively new to those working in schools, it offers the potential and possibility for sustained improvement. The simple but compelling idea that 'all teachers can lead' is central to successful school improvement. Barth (1990) argues that if schools are going to become places in which all children are learning then *all teachers must be leaders*. He suggests *that all teachers harbour leadership capabilities waiting to be unlocked and engaged for the good of the school* (emphasis added).

The critical question therefore is *how* to enhance and develop teacher leadership in schools. While answers may be easy to locate, they are much more difficult to implement. As this book has shown where teachers feel *involved* and *skilled* in leadership activity, then their leadership capability is extended. Similarly, where teachers learn from one another through mentoring, observation, peer coaching and mutual reflection, the possibilities of generating teacher leadership are significantly enhanced. Investing in the school as a *learning community* offers the greatest opportunity to unlock leadership capabilities and capacities among teachers.

The rate and nature of change in the twenty-first century will necessitate new and alternative approaches to school improvement and school leadership. If schools are to be real learning communities this cannot be achieved by operating with outdated models of change and improvement dependent upon individual leadership. Developing and sustaining school improvement will require schools to invest in and nurture the leadership capabilities of all those within their school community. Sustainability *begs for a rhythm or dance of development* (Lambert 2002: 157) generated through developing the leadership capacity and capability of *all* those within a school community.

The theme of this book is a simple one. Teachers are of paramount importance in helping schools to improve and to build the capacity to sustain improvement. However, as we have seen, building capacity requires deep-rooted organizational change and a fundamental shift in thinking about leadership practices. The process of capacity building is inherently messy, emotionally fraught and complex. But it is not impossible. Releasing the potential of every teacher to lead is the first step in building the capacity for school improvement. The route to sustainable school improvement is as simple and complex as that.

APPENDIX A: LEADERSHIP CAPACITY SURVEY

CAPACITY SURVEY

Teachers' self- and colleague-assessment form

This is an assessment of leadership dispositions, knowledge and skills needed to build leadership capacity in schools and organizations. The items are clustered by the characteristics of schools with high leadership capacity. It may be completed by a school teacher or by a colleague who is familiar with the work of that teacher. The survey information is most useful if completed by two colleagues and the teacher him- or herself. To the right of each item is a Liker-type scale: NO = not observed, IP = infrequently performed, FP = frequently performed, CP = consistently performed, CTO = can teach to others. Please complete the scale for each item.

A Broad-based involvement in the work of leadership	NO	IP	FP	CP	CTO
1 Assist in the establishment of representative governance and work groups.					
2 Organize the school to maximize interactions among all school community members.					
3 Share authority and resources broadly.					
4 Engage others in opportunities to lead.					

B Skilful involvement in the work of leadership	NO	IP	FP	CP	CTO
1 Model, describe, demonstrate the following leadership skills:					
a develop shared purposes of learning					
b facilitate group processes					
c communicate (especially listening and questioning)					
d reflection on practice					
e enquiry into the questions and issues confronting your school community					
f collaborative planning					
g conflict management among adults					
h problem solving with colleagues and pupils					
i managing change and transitions					
j constructivist learning designs for pupils and adults					
2 Communicate through action and words the relationship between leadership and learning.					

C Enquiry-based use of information to inform shared decisions and practice	NO	IP	FP	CP	CTO
1 Engage with others in a learning cycle (reflection, dialogue, question posing, enquiry, construction of meaning, planned action)					
2 Develop plans and schedules for the creation of shared time for dialogue and reflection.					
3 Identify, discover and interpret information and school data/evidence.					
4 Design and implement a communication system that keeps all informed and involved in securing and interpretating of data.					
5 Participate with others in shared governance processes that integrate data into decision making.					

D Roles and responsibilities reflect broad involvement and collaboration	NO	IP	FP	CP	CTO
1 Own role includes attention to the classroom, the school, the community and the profession.					
2 Observe and be sensitive to indicators that participants are performing outside traditional roles. Give feedback to participants regarding the benefit of these changes.					
3 Develop strategies for strengthening the new relationships that will emerge from broaden roles.					
4 Develop mutual expectations and strategies for ensuring that participants share responsibility for the implementation of school community agreements.					

E Reflective practice/innovation is the norm	NO	IP	FP	CP	CTO
1 Ensure that the cycle of enquiry and time schedules involve a continuous and ongoing reflective phase.					
2 Demonstrate and encourage individual and group initiative by providing access to resources, personnel, time and outside networks.					
3 Practise and support innovation without expectations for early success.					
4 Encourage and participate in collaborative innovation.					
5 Engage with other innovators in developing own criteria for monitoring, assessment and accountability regarding own individual and shared work.					

F Pupil achievement is high	NO	IP	FP	CP	CTO
1 Work with members of the school community to establish challenging and humane expectations and standards.					
2 Design, teach, coach and assess authentic curriculum, instruction and performance-based assessment processes that ensure that all children learn.					
3 Provide systematic feedback to children and families about pupil progress					
4 Receive feedback about family learning expectations.					
5 Redesign roles and structures to enable the school to develop and sustain resiliency in children (e.g. teacher as coach/counsellor/mentor).					
6 Ensure that the learning cycle within the school includes evidence from performance-based assessment, examination of pupil work and research.					

Scoring: Summarize the number of responses in each category of characteristics in three broad groups (NO and IP; FP and CP; CTO):

E Reflective practice/innovation is the norm	NO	IP	FP	CP	CTO
A Broad-based involvement in the work of leadership					
B Skilful involvement in the work of leadership					
C Enquiry-based use of information to inform shared decisions and practice					
D Roles and responsibilities reflect broad involvement and collaboration					
E Reflective practice/innovation is the norm					
F Pupil achievement is high					
Suggested: Note each area in your professional development plans, and in:					
NO/IP areas – find opportunities to observe these behaviours, participate in specific training. FP/CP areas – find more opportunities to demonstrate and practise. CTO areas – find opportunities to teach and coach others, participate in formal governance groups.					

APPENDIX B: A RUBRIC FOR ASSESSING

TEACHER LEADERSHIP

A Adult development

1 Defines self in relation to others in the community. The opinions of others, particularly those in authority, are highly important.	• Defines self as independent from the group, separating needs and goals from others. Does not often see the need for group action.	• Understands self as interdependent with others in the school community, seeking feedback from others and counsel from self.	• Engages colleagues in acting out of a sense of self and shared values, forming interdependent learning communities.
2 Does not yet recognize the need for self-reflection. Tends to implement strategies as learned without making adjustments arising from reflective practice.	• Personal reflection leads to refinement of strategies and routines. Does not often share reflections with others. Focuses on argument for own ideas. Does not support systems which are designed to enhance reflective practice.	• Engages in self-reflection as a means of improving practices. Models these processes for others in the school community. Holds conversations that share views and develops understanding of each other's assumptions.	• Evokes reflection in others. Develops and supports a culture for self-reflection that may include collaborative planning, peer coaching, action research and reflective writing.

3 Absence of ongoing evaluation of their teaching. Does not yet systematically connect teacher and student behaviours.	• Self-evaluation is not often shared with others; however, responsibility for problems or errors is typically ascribed to others such as students or family.	• Highly self-evaluative and introspective. Accepts shared responsibility as a natural part of a school community. No need for blame.	• Enables others to be self-evaluative and introspective, leading towards self- and shared-responsibility.
4 In need of effective strategies to demonstrate respect and concern for others. Is polite, yet primarily focuses on own needs.	• Exhibits respectful attitude towards others in most situations, usually privately. Can be disrespectful in public debate. Gives little feedback to others.	• Consistently shows respect and concern for all members of the school community. Validates and respects qualities in and opinions of others.	• Encourages and supports others in being respectful, caring, trusted members of the school community. Initiates recognition of the ideas and achievements of colleagues as part of an overall goal of collegial empowerment.

B Dialogue

1 Interactions with others are primarily social, not based on common goals or group learning.	• Communicates with others around logistical issues/problems. Sees goals as individually set for each classroom, not actively participating in efforts to focus on common goals.	• Communicates well with individuals and groups in the community as a means of creating and sustaining relationships and focusing on teaching and learning. Actively participates in dialogue.	• Facilitates effective dialogue among members of the school community in order to build relationships and focus the dialogue on teaching and learning.

2 Does not pose questions of or seek to influence the group. Participation often resembles consent or compliance.	• Makes personal point of view, although not assumptions, explicit. When opposed to ideas, often asks questions which can derail or divert the dialogue.	• Asks questions and provides insights that reflect an understanding of the need to surface assumptions and address the goals of the community.	• Facilitates communication among colleagues by asking provocative questions which open productive dialogue.
3 Does not actively seek information or new professional knowledge which challenges current practices. Shares knowledge with others only when requested.	• Attends staff development activities that are planned by the school or LEA. Occasionally shares knowledge during formal and informal gatherings. Does not seek knowledge that challenges status quo.	• Possesses current knowledge and information about teaching and learning. Actively seeks to use that understanding to alter teaching practices. Studies own practice.	• Works with others to construct knowledge through multiple forms of enquiry, action research, examination of disaggregated school data, insights from others and from the outside research community.
4 Responds to situations in similar ways; expects predictable responses from others. Is sometimes confused by variations from expected norms.	• Responds to situations in different, although predictable ways. Expects consistency from those in authority and from self.	• Responds to situations with an open-mind and flexibility; welcomes multiple perspectives from others. Alters own assumptions during dialogue when evidence is persuasive.	• Promotes an open-mind and flexibility in others; invites multiple perspectives and interpretations as a means of challenging old assumptions and framing new actions.

C Collaboration

1 Decision making is based on individual wants and needs rather than those of the group as a whole.	• Promotes individual autonomy in classroom decision making. Relegates school decision making to the principal.	• Actively participates in shared decision making. Volunteers to follow through on group decisions.	• Promotes collaborative decision making that provides options to meet the diverse individual and group needs of the school community.
2 Sees little value in team building, although seeks membership in the group. Will participate, although does not connect activities with larger school goals.	• Does not seek to participate in roles or settings that would involve team building. Considers most team-building activities to be 'touchy-feely' and frivolous.	• Is an active participant in team building, seeking roles and opportunities to contribute to the work of the team. Sees 'teamness' as central to community.	• Engages colleagues in team-building activities that develop mutual trust and promotes collaborative decision making.
3 Sees problems as caused by the actions of others, e.g. students, parents, or blames self. Uncertain regarding the specifics of one's own involvement.	• Interprets problems from own perspective. Plays the role of observer and critic, not accepting responsibility for emerging issues and dilemmas. Considers most problems to be a function of poor management.	• Acknowledges that problems involve all members of the community. Actively seeks to define problems and proposes resolutions or approaches which address the situation. Finding blame is not relevant.	• Engages colleagues in identifying and acknowledging problems. Acts with others to frame problems and seek problem resolutions. Anticipates situations which may cause recurrent problems.

(4) Avoids	Engages	Anticipates	Surfaces/mediates
4 Does not recognize or avoids conflict in the school community. Misdirects frustrations into withdrawal or personal hurt. Avoids talking about issues that could evoke conflict.	• Does not shy away from conflict. Engages in conflict as a means of surfacing competing ideas, approaches. Understands that conflict is intimidating to many.	• Anticipates and seeks to resolve or intervene in conflict. Actively tries to channel conflict into problem-solving endeavours. Is not intimidated by conflict, although would not seek it.	• Surfaces, addresses and mediates conflict within the school and with parents and community. Understands that negotiating conflict is necessary for personal and school change.

D Organizational change

1 Focuses on present situations and issues; seldom plans for either short- or long-term futures. Expects certainty.	• Demonstrates forward thinking for own classroom. Usually does not connect own planning to the future of the school.	• Develops forward thinking skills in working with others and planning for school improvements. Future goals based on common values and vision.	• Provides for and creates opportunities to engage others in forward (visionary) thinking and planning based on common core values.
2 Maintains a low profile during school change, basically uninvolved in group processes. Attempts to comply with changes. Expects compliance from others.	• Questions status quo; suggests that others need to change in order to improve it. Selects those changes which reflect personal philosophies. Opposes or ignores practices which require a school-wide focus.	• Shows enthusiasm and involvement in school change. Leads by example. Explores possibilities and implements changes for both personal and professional development.	• Initiates actions towards innovative change; motivates and draws others into the action for school and LEA improvements. Encourages others to implement practices which support school-wide learning. Provides follow-up planning and coaching support.

3 Culturally unaware. 'I treat everyone the same'. Stage of naivety to socio-political implications of race, culture, ethnic and gender issues.	• Growing sensitivity to political implications of diversity. Acknowledges that cultural differences exist and influence individuals and organizations.	• Acceptance and understanding . . . 'aha' level. Has developed an appreciation of own cultural identities and a deeper appreciation/respect for cultural differences. Applies understanding in classroom and school.	• Commitment to value of and build on cultural differences. Actively seeks to involve others in designing programmes and policies which support the development of a multi-cultural world.
4 Attends to students in his or her own classroom. Possessive of children and space. Has not yet secured a developmental view of children.	• Concerned for the preparation of children in previous grades. Critical of preparation of children and readiness of children to meet established standards.	• Developmental view of children translates into concern for all children in the school (not only those in own classroom) and their future performances in further educational settings.	• Works with colleagues to develop programmes and policies that take holistic view of children's development (e.g. multi-graded classrooms, multi-year teacher assignments, parent education, follow-up studies).
5 Works alongside new teachers, is cordial although does not offer assistance. Lacks confidence in giving feedback to others.	• Shares limited information with new teachers, mainly that which pertains to administrative functions in the school (e.g. attendance accounting, grade reports). Does not offer to serve as a master teacher.	• Collaborates with, supports and gives feedback to new and student teachers. Often serves as master teacher.	• Takes responsibility for the support and development of systems for new and student teachers. Develops collaborative programmes with school, LEA and universities.

6 Displays little interest in the selection of new teachers. Assumes that they will be appointed by the LEA or those otherwise in authority.

• Assumes that LEA will recruit and appoint teachers. Has not proposed a more active role to the teachers' association.

• Becomes actively involved in the setting of criteria and the selection of new teachers.

• Advocates to the schools, LEA and teachers' association the development of hiring practices that involve teachers, parents and students in the processes. Promotes the hiring of diversity candidates.

REFERENCES

Barth, R. (1990) *Improving Schools From Within: Teachers, Parent and Principals can Make a Difference*. San Francisco: Jossey Bass.

Clarke, P. (2002) *Learning Schools, Learning Systems*. London: Continuum Press.

Creemers, B. (1994) *The Effective Classroom*. London: Cassell.

Day, C., Harris, A., Hadfield, M., Tolley, H. and Beresford, J. (2000) *Leading Schools in Times of Change*. Buckingham: Milton Keynes Open University Press.

Fullan, M. (1999) *Change Forces: The Sequel*. Buckingham: Open University Press.

Fullan, M. (2001) *Leading in a Culture of Change*. San Francisco, CA: Jossey Bass.

Goleman, D. (2002) *The New Leaders: Transforming the Art of Leadership into the Science of Results*. London: Little Brown.

Hadfield, M. and Chapman, C. (2002) *Building Leadership Capacity*, Report, National College for School Leadership. Nottingham.

Hargreaves, A. *et al.* (2001) *Learning to Change: Teaching Beyond Subjects and Standards.* San Francisco: Jossey-Bass.

Hargreaves, D. (1995) School culture, school effectiveness and school improvement, *School Effectiveness and School Improvement*, 6(1): 23–46.

Harris, A. (2001) Building the capacity for school improvement, *School Leadership and Management*, 21(3): 261–70.

Harris, A. (2002a) *School Improvement: What's in it for Schools?* London: Routledge/Falmer.

Harris, A. (2002b) *Leading the Improving Department.* London: David Fulton Press.

Harris, A. and Chapman, C. (2002) *Leadership in Schools Facing Challenging Circumstances*, Report, National College for School Leadership. Nottingham.

Harris, A. and Crispeels, J. (eds) (forthcoming) *International Perspectives on School Improvement.* Lisse: Swets and Zeitlinger.

Harris, A., Day, C., Hadfield, M., Hopkins, D., Hargreaves, A. and Chapman, C. (2003) *Effective Leadership for School Improvement.* London: Routledge/Falmer.

Hopkins, D. (2001) *School Improvement for Real.* London: Falmer Press.

Hopkins, D. and Harris, A. (2001) *Creating the Conditions for Classroom Improvement.* London: David Fulton Press.

Hopkins, D. and Jackson, D. (2002) Building the capacity for reading and learning, in A. Harris *et al.*, *Effective Leadership for School Improvement.* London: Routledge.

Hopkins, D. *et al.* (2002) *Improving the Quality of Education for All.* London: David Fulton Press.

Lambert, L. (1998) *Building Leadership Capacity in Schools.* Alexandria, VA: Association for Supervision and Curriculum Development.

Lambert, L. (2002) *Developing Sustainable Leadership Capacity in Schools and Districts.* Alexandria, VA: Association for Supervision and Curriculum Development.

Lambert, L., Kent, K., Richert, A.E., Collay, M. and Dietz, M.E. (1997) *Who Will Save Our Schools? Teachers as Constructivist Leaders.* Thousand Oaks, CA: Corwin Press.

Lambert, L., Walker, D., Zimmerman, D. *et al.* (1998) *The Constructivist Leader.* New York: Teachers College Press.

Little, J.W. (1993) Teachers professional development in a climate of educational reform, *Educational Evaluation and Policy Analysis*, 15(2): 129–51.

Mitchell, C. and Sackney, L. (2000) *Profound Improvement: Building Capacity for a Learning Community*. Downington, PA: Lisse, Swets and Zeitlinger.

National College for School Leadership (2001) *Leadership Framework*. Nottingham: NCSL.

Senge, P. (1990) *The Fifth Discipline: The Art and Practice of the Learning Organisation*. New York: Doubleday.

Sergiovanni, T. (2000) *The Lifeworld of Leadership*. London: Jossey Bass.

Sergiovanni, T. (2001) *Leadership: What's in it for Schools?* London: Routledge/Falmer.

Stoll, L. and Myers, K. (1998) *No Quick Fixes: Perspectives on Schools in Difficulty*.

Wenger, E. (1998) *Communities of Practice: Learning, Meaning and Identity*. Cambridge: Cambridge University Press.

INDEX

LEADING SCHOOLS IN TIMES OF CHANGE

Christopher Day, Alma Harris, Mark Hadfield, Harry Tolley and John Beresford

... a refreshing and rigorous, evidence-based view of the challenges, joys and headaches of being a successful headteacher ...

> Mick Brookes, President,
> National Association of Headteachers

... a significant contribution to our understanding of the qualities those in, and aspiring to, school leader roles need to possess and to further develop.

> Kenneth Leithwood, Centre for Leadership Development,
> OISE, University of Toronto

... a superbly balanced book at the cutting edge of writing on school leadership.

Brian Caldwell, Dean of Education, University of Melbourne

A must read for anyone serious about improving schools.

> Thomas J. Sergiovanni, Lillian Radford Professor of
> Education and Administration at Trinity University, USA

Leadership of schools in changing times is fraught with opportunities and challenges. This book considers effective leadership and management of schools from the perspectives of headteachers, teachers, students, ancillaries, governors and parents in a variety of reputationally good schools of different phases, locations and sizes. Through a mixture of participants' accounts and analysis of leadership theory, this highly readable book reveals a number of characteristics of headteachers who are both effective and successful: the centrality of personal values, people-centred leadership and the ability to manage tensions and dilemmas. The authors propose a post-transformational theory that reflects the complexity of leadership behaviour in the twenty-first century, suggesting that reliance upon rational, managerialist theory as the basis for training is inappropriate for the values-led contingency model that is necessary to lead schools successfully in times of change.

Contents

Introduction – The changing face of headship – Studying leadership in schools from multiple perspectives – The headteachers – The deputies and teachers – The perspectives of governors, parents and support staff – The students' perspectives – School leadership: tensions and dilemmas – Post-transformational leadership – References – Index.

224pp   0 335 20582 8 (Paperback)   0 335 20583 6 (Hardback)

EDUCATIONAL LEADERSHIP AND LEARNING
PRACTICE, POLICY AND RESEARCH

Sue Law and Derek Glover

> . . . it sets out both the theory and the everyday realities that
> lie behind the Government's 'improving leadership' agenda.
>
> *T.E.S. Friday*

Educational leaders – whether in schools, colleges or higher education – are challenged with steering unprecedented change; educational management has never been more demanding. Within
the context of a new 'learning age' and the Teacher Training
Agency's National Standards, this book explores many of the key
issues facing those both aspiring to and already involved in leadership and management, whether at middle or senior levels.

While focusing particularly on schools and colleges, this book
evaluates issues increasingly central to leadership in a variety of
professional educational settings, for example, school improvement, innovation, teamwork, organizational culture, professional
development, motivation and the nature of leadership. In identifying key concepts, it scrutinizes possible management strategies
within a changing policy context that is increasingly focused
around standards, accountability and reputation.

The book utilizes research evidence to illuminate the practices,
challenges and problems facing educationists and endeavours to
overcome the perceived gap between practice and research to create an integrated approach to leadership and management development: one which both supports and stimulates managers' professional development aspirations.

Contents
*Part I Leading and managing – The context for educational lead-
ership – Developing leadership and management effectiveness –
Managing ourselves and leading others – Motivating and managing others – Leading effective teams – Part II Changing and
learning – Effective communication – Organizational cultures –
Managing change and creating opportunities – Educational
improvement, inspection and effectiveness – Leading and managing in learning organizations – Part III Tasks and responsibilities – Managing staff and promoting quality – Managing
resources and finance – Managing stakeholder relationships and
partnerships – Leading and managing for professional development – Postscript – Bibliography – Name index – Subject index.*

320pp   0 335 19752 3 (Paperback)   0 335 19753 1 (Hardback)